introducing japan

History
Way of life
Creative world
Seen & heard
Food & wine

ST. MARTIN'S PRESS   NEW YORK

edited by Paul Norbury

Copyright © 1977 by Paul Norbury Publications Ltd.
All rights reserved. For information, write:
St. Martin's Press, Inc., 175 Fifth Ave., New York, N.Y. 10010
Printed in Great Britain
Library of Congress Catalog Card Number: 77-3853
First published in the United States of America in 1978

Library of Congress Cataloging in Publication Data

Main entry under title:

Introducing Japan.

    Selections from Tsuru.
    1. Japan—Addresses, essays, lectures. I. Norbury,
Paul. II. Tsuru.
DS806.I57   952   77-3853
ISBN 0-312-42542-2

Design coordination by Martin Causer

Life is not measured by a tale of days
Or months or years, but by the experience
We garner from our opportunities.

From *A Japanese Don Juan* by John Paris, 1926

Contents

4 Seen and heard

5 Food and wine

List of illustrations

Editor's Preface

In referring to the stringent demands that Nature exacts from the rock-laden islands of Japan by way of volcanoes, typhoons and earthquakes, the writer William MacQuitty says later in these pages that in spite of such daunting circumstances, the Japanese are able to take advantage of the inevitable and like their oysters turn their liabilities into pearls. In 1970 I felt very much a liability in agreeing to edit and produce Europe's first popular quarterly about Japan and the Japanese. The journal was to be called *Tsuru*, Japanese for the flying crane and emblem of Japan's national carrier whose offspring it was to be.

My schooling in the fifties had taught me nothing about the 'cherry blossom land' or its people, and I can't remember even uttering the word

Japan to my own students during my two years in teaching. Like many others of my generation my views reflected the commonly held stereotyped images of Japan unsubstantiated by any direct knowledge or experience. Even as the sixties got under way, I can only recall comments about low-priced Japanese goods and inscrutable businessmen. And since I was not a motor-bike enthusiast, camera buff or hi-fi afficionado, the names Yamaha, Nikon and Sony simply didn't register.

What did, however, were conversations with a colleague at Esso Europe Inc., where I was working in the late sixties, who had previously been with the company in the Far East and knew Japan. In the things he liked and discussed his interest in them was often contagious, packaged as it was in a lyrical Kentucky drawl. I decided I would like to visit Japan someday.

One of those odd things was the fact that my Esso office was located directly over the Japan Air Lines ticket office in Hanover Square. Even odder was the fact that within the year I was to be sitting at a desk in another company trying to rationalize a master plan for a new magazine about Japan, to be published by the very airline I had nonchalantly rubbed shoulders with in the Square.

I like to think that my success in obtaining the appointment was partly due to a certain journalistic and editorial competence, but also because of my great interest in the professional challenge of communicating what seemed to me one of the world's most bewildering and confusing industrialized societies, and one that by 1970 was demanding increasingly the attention of the world.

As I began the task of formulating *Tsuru,* I reflected on the miniaturized version of the famous Rioan-ji stone and raked sand garden in Kyoto on display in the JAL ticket office — something I had passed numerous times but never once stopped to discover what it was, or what it meant, or what sort of people had created it. The great host of leading writers that subsequently contributed to *Tsuru* gradually unravelled the mystery. They put the Japanese people under the microscope of their wide experience and expertise and opened so many windows on the structure and culture of this remarkable island race. They turned over the stones of Rioan-ji and revealed the lining and the ground plan. I fondly imagine they turned the liability I represented into a pearl.

The pearl was *Tsuru**. This book has enabled me to put its best qualities on permanent display.

As well as the writers, photographers and illustrators who collectively have made this book, I am indebted to a great host of people for their inspiration and support from the days when *Tsuru* was in print to the present time. But I must express special thanks to my wife and family who watched me fly East so many times on my voyage of discovery; to Derek Birdsall, designer, for his flair and friendship and who shared with me the agony and ecstasy of publishing; to the staff of Westerham Press for their skills in the art of the possible; and to the many people with whom I worked individually at Japan Air Lines both in London and Tokyo for their critical interest and enthusiasm and for graciously putting up with their recalcitrant editor.

Paul Norbury
September 1976

*Tsuru was published over a four-year period, closing in January 1975. It was produced in four separate language editions, English, French, German and Italian and for a time in Spanish. It had a named readership of 26,000 and found its way to most corners of the world. It won a major British design award in 1973 and published the writings and pictures of over sixty authors, photographers and illustrators.

Frank Ashton-Gwatkin who died in 1976 at the age of 86, wrote a number of novels including *Banzai* and *Kimono* under the pen-name of John Paris. After his Japan Consular service, 1913–19 he specialized in Far Eastern affairs at the Foreign Office and later worked with Arnold Toynbee at the Royal Institute of International Affairs.

Geoffrey Bownas is Professor of Japanese and Director of the Centre of Japanese Studies at the University of Sheffield. He specialises in the economic and social developments of modern Japan. His published works include *The Penguin Book of Japanese Verse* (with Anthony Thwaite), *New Writing in Japan* (with Yukio Mishima) and *Business in Japan* (with Paul Norbury).

David Chibbett is Assistant Keeper of Oriental Scrolls and Manuscripts at the British Library and is a Japan specialist and translator. His published translations include *The Japan-China Phenomenon* by Shuichi Kato and he has recently completed his own study of the history of Japanese printing. He is currently working on a history of Japanese literature by Shuichi Kato to be published jointly by Macmillan and Paul Norbury Publications in 1977.

Michael Cooper S. J. is editor of *Monumenta Nipponica* published by Sophia University, Tokyo and considered to be one of the most scholarly reviews of its kind on Japan. His published works include *They Came to Japan, The Southern Barbarians* and *Rodrigues*. He has been in Japan since 1954.

Charles Dunn is Reader in Japanese at the School of Oriental and African Studies, University of London. He has lived and travelled extensively in Japan, and his researches into *Kabuki* and Japanese puppet drama have been widely acclaimed. His published works include *Everyday Life in Traditional Japan*.

Tony Dyson is a businessman working with Commercial Union. He made Japan his speciality and for seven years successfully built up the company's business in Osaka and Tokyo. His pictures of Japan have been published in various journals including the Daily Telegraph Weekend Supplement. He returned to England in 1975.

Jun Eto is a leading Japanese literary critic and is Associate Professor of Sociology at the Tokyo University of Technology. He has travelled extensively to the West and gives frequent lectures. In 1970 he was awarded the Shincho Literary Prize and the Noma Literary Prize for his book *Soseki and His Times*.

Jill Gribbin has lived in Japan for a number of years. She is an expert in Japanese antiques, and has studied traditional Japanese dance. She lectures and writes regularly about Japan. Before returning to Japan in 1976 she was editor of the Japan Society of London Bulletin. Her husband, David, is an advertising consultant and has himself written numerous articles on doing business in Japan.

John Grisdale is a poet, artist and writer and has lived many years in Japan. He is the author of a great many articles on Japan in numerous journals as well as a successful exhibitor of his paintings. He returned to Britain in 1976 to pursue his Japan interests. He published a collection of his poems entitled *Poet's Salter* in 1975.

Nobutoshi Hagihara is a journalist, broadcaster and political historian who has travelled extensively in Europe and studied at St Antony's College, Oxford. He is currently living in Tokyo.

Shuichi Kato is one of Japan's leading literary figures with wide-ranging interests in sociology and international affairs. He has been a visiting professor at a number of leading western universities including those of Munich, Berlin, British Columbia and Yale. He is currently Professor of International Affairs at Sophia University, Tokyo. His published works in English include *Form, Style, Tradition* and *The Japan-China Phenomenon*. He has recently published in Japanese a definitive history of Japanese literature.

Bernard Keeffe is a singer, actor, writer and freelance conductor and broadcaster who speaks fluent Japanese and has made numerous visits to Japan in his professional capacity. He was formerly head of the BBC's Radio-opera and later became the BBC's staff conductor of the Scottish Symphony Orchestra.

Irma Kurtz, an American living in Britain, has won wide acclaim for her incisive writing and reporting on a great many subjects for a wide cross-section of newspapers and publications. She also does freelance work on radio and TV and travels extensively.

Anthony Lawrence, formerly the BBC's correspondent in Hong Kong has come to know Japan in a long association of over 20 years. He established a reputation worldwide for the insight, sensitivity and thoroughness he brought to his reporting. He continues to work freelance in Hong Kong and his published works include *Our Own Correspondent*.

Notes on Contributors

Bernard Leach is the first western potter to have studied the technique of Far Eastern pottery in Japan and Korea. Born in Hong Kong in 1887, he learned the craft of pottery in Japan under the representative of the sixth generation of the Kenzan school and went on to inspire both Kenkichi Tomimoto and Shoji Hamada to become potters. His pottery is in St Ives, Cornwall, and his many books include *A Potter in Japan* and *Kenzan and His Tradition*. He was decorated with the Order of the Sacred Treasure, second class, in 1966.

Jean-Pierre Lehmann, a Frenchman, is a lecturer in Japanese and Chinese history at the University of Stirling, Scotland. He has made a speciality of Franco-Japanese relations and has recently completed research on Bakamatsu politics and the Roches controversy. He spent much of his childhood in Japan and is a regular visitor today.

William MacQuitty is a Fellow of the Royal Geographical Society, and an extensively travelled writer and photographer. His very successful book on *Abu Simbel* (1965) arose from his direct involvement in the plans to save the temples. Other published works include *Buddha*, *Great Botanical Gardens of the World* and *Tutankamen*.

Fosco Maraini who lives in Florence has been intimately associated with Japan for the past thirty years as a distinguished writer, photographer and scholar. He has recently completed a study of the Ainu in northern Japan. His published works include *Meeting With Japan* and *Japan: Patterns of Continuity*.

Chie Nakane is a Professor of Social Anthropology at the Institute of Oriental Culture, University of Tokyo. She is recognised as one of Japan's leading sociologists. Her book *Japanese Society* has become a standard work on the subject. She takes part in numerous international conventions and is a regular speaker.

P. G. O'Neill is a Professor of Japanese at the School of Oriental and African Studies, University of London. He is an acknowledged expert on the structure of the Japanese language and has also specialised on *Nō* and Japanese folklore. His published works include *Essential Kanji, Early Nō Drama* and *Japanese Names*.

Charles Parr is a freelance journalist and travel writer who is a regular visitor to Japan. He writes for a wide range of travel journals and publishes regularly in the leading British daily and Sunday newspapers.

Richard Storry is Director of the Far East Centre and Fellow of St Antony's College, Oxford. He spent several years in Japan as a college lecturer prior to the second world war and has since revisited the country many times. He is today one of Britain's leading historians and commentators on Japan. His published works include *The Penguin History of Modern Japan* and *Mirror, Sword and Jewel (ed)*.

Arnold Toynbee who died in 1975, was for thirty years Director of Studies at the Royal Institute of International Affairs, London, and Research Professor of International History at the University of London. He was a member of the British delegations at the Paris peace conference of both 1919 and 1946. He was a prolific writer, best known, perhaps, for his 12-volume *A Study of History*. He was awarded the Order of the Sacred Treasure, first class, by the Japanese Government in 1969.

Fritz Vos is Professor of Japanese and Korean at the University of Leiden, Holland, with a special interest in pre-Meiji Japan. He is one of Holland's leading commentators on Japan and has published numerous extracts and books.

Ken Wlaschin, an American, is Programme Director at the National Film Theatre with a special interest in the Italian and Japanese cinema. He writes regularly for the British journal "Films and Filming" and has also published a novel and a guidebook to Rome.

Kenichi Yoshida is one of Japan's foremost literary critics and writers; he is a leading authority on Shakespeare as well as a translator of various French and English classics. He is the son of former prime minister, Shigeru Yoshida, and he was for a time at the University of Cambridge. His first book in English *Japan is a Circle* was published by Paul Norbury Publications in 1975.

東京名所
日本橋
京橋之間
鉄道馬車
往復之図

1 Historical perspective

Japan: through a glass darkly
by David G. Chibbett

In economic terms, Japan is, today, one of the world's leading nations. That is indisputable. Yet despite the efforts of several generations of American and European scholars to explain and interpret Japanese civilization, there is no doubt that in the general public view Japan remains a little understood country, though we are at last seeing a far greater coverage by the media than ever before. In many ways it is not surprising that this lack of understanding should exist. Much less than a hundred and fifty years ago, Japan, to all intents and purposes, did not exist at all in the western view of things and despite a steady century of progress towards the fringe of super-power status, there are still many barriers against a proper western understanding of Japan and the Japanese.

Foremost among these is the barrier of language, for there are still comparatively very few Europeans and Americans with sufficient knowledge to read books in Japanese about the culture and civilization of Japan, and Japanese efforts to explain themselves in European languages have not been noticeably successful.

Even westerners with sufficient knowledge have been reluctant to commit themselves about subjects such as Japanese literature, which is one of the reasons why translations of novels, a comparatively straightforward process, have been made in such numbers whereas the number of books *about* literature are very few indeed.

There is still a marked feeling among western scholars of Japan that they are not really in a position to judge Japanese civilization, although it is certainly true that they have proved themselves far more objective than native scholars of Japanese culture.

Allied to the barrier of language, there is the barrier of distance, because although rapid advances in communications have taken place during the last thirty years, few westerners have the opportunity to visit Japan for themselves and see how their preconceived ideas accord with reality.

Thus the popular view of Japan remains a strange blend of awareness of the hard facts of economic power and romantic notions of *geisha* girls, the tea ceremony, flower arrangement, *judo* and the *kimono*. It is also true that the war and the atom bomb continue to loom large in British and American memories in particular, although this will gradually cease to be so as the war generation dies out. The romantic notion of Japan will die much harder, not least because the Japanese actively foster it as being good for tourism.

Although Japan has a long (but broken) history of relations with the West dating back to the sixteenth century, it is only during and after the last war that the Japanese have really forced themselves on the attention of the world. It is true that westerners have a vague and far from perfect understanding of the Japanese, but the nature of cultural relations is such that, in all probability, the Japanese have an equally uncertain understanding of the West — despite the fact that Japan has been the only Asian country to compete with the West successfully on its own terms. Let's examine this situation more closely.

The basic social character of the modern Japanese was formed during the self-imposed isolation of the Edo period (1603-1868). During the 1630s, the Japanese expelled the Spanish and Portuguese traders and missionaries (who had arrived about ninety years before) for fear of invasion by the countries they represented, and were to have no substantial contact with the West until the period following the American Commodore Perry's 're-opening Japan' expedition in the summer of 1853.

During the first hundred years of contact, the Japanese were able to follow their time-honoured policy of selectivity in cultural relations, if such a positive word as 'policy' can be applied to the basically haphazard process of cultural assimilation. Protected by their geographical position, the Japanese until the modern period were able to stave off any foreign invasion with little difficulty and thus could adopt from foreign civilizations only what they chose to adopt.

Interestingly, during the early contacts with the nations of Western Europe, the Japanese were concerned not so much with their visitors' cultural attainments as with their technical accomplishments. Indeed, except for the vague menace of western power which was to haunt the authorities throughout the period of the 'closed country', it is probable that this early European influence was severely localized and short lived.

The Japanese were certainly very curious even if only out of superficial interest, about the habits and physical appearance of the Europeans as is demonstrated by the fact that Dutch sightseers in Nagasaki (throughout the closed period the Dutch were allowed to maintain a small trading-post on the island of Deshima in Nagasaki harbour) became a common theme in Japanese art, particularly in the 1800s.

The isolation imposed on Japan by the Tokugawa government after the expulsion of the Europeans was to have a decisive effect not only on Japan's relations with foreign countries, but also on the very character of the people. The government during the period of seclusion was autocratic, the people not being allowed to travel very much, even within Japan, and forced into an obedience to a form of caste system. In other words, it was during this period that two of the most noticeable features of the modern Japanese emerged — obedience to authority and identification with the group. Individuality, never a very strong trait, was ruthlessly suppressed.

When, separately and jointly, the Americans, British, Dutch, French and Germans forced Japan into the modern world during the 1850s and 1860s, there existed all the makings of a major political and cultural conflict. Essentially individualistic, western civilization had trampled its way across the world during the eighteenth and nineteenth centuries, meeting with few reverses. Geographical position was no longer a protection for the Japanese and it is certain that if they had chosen to resist the West, Japan would have met the same fate that China had met — partition. That the Japanese survived the West's incursions and prospered was due to the fact that instead of resisting the power of the West, they strove to emulate it.

In terms of the nineteenth century, to secure parity with the western powers meant achieving equality in the things the West valued most, namely economic and military power. One of the major reasons why Japan was able to do this as quickly as she did was due to a very real difference of attitude towards the West from that of, say, the Chinese. Although well aware of their own long cultural tradition, the Japanese did not regard the westerners as in any sense inferior or as 'barbarians'. The Japanese word *gaijin*, applied to foreigners indiscriminately, actually means 'outsider' and is not in itself derogatory. Thus they felt no sense of incongruity in importing a whole host of different institutions, political, military and economic, from the West and manoeuvring them into the Japanese system.

Many of the importations of course were incongruous and alien to the historical character of the nation. For a time, swamped by a willing acceptance of the full powers of western industrialized society and civilization, the Japanese were caught between two forces. On the one hand there was a mad passion for all things western (typified in a minor way by the Japanese engineers, who in the full flood of enthusiasm for western methods, went round the country throwing up huge iron girder bridges over the smallest and most insignificant streams). This was eventually followed by a fierce nationalistic reaction in favour of tradition. The incongruities of the imposition of western civilization on the institutions of Japan permeated the whole of society, and in many ways the Japanese, for a time, lost their sense of national identity. It could be argued that they still have not found it, and this, perhaps, is the tragedy of modern Japan.

It seems fairly certain that general public consciousness of Japan in the West dates from the Second World War which also marks an interesting turning point in the Japanese view of the West. Confronted with a complex background of political, social and psychological factors, the Japanese embarked on the process of building themselves an empire.

Much has been written about the Pacific war and in particular about the cruelty the Japanese displayed during the course of it. This is an important aspect of the war which needs explanation if only because it is this very thing that many westerners associate with Japan. The Japanese had fought two minor wars against China in 1894-5 and Russia in 1904-5, but the Pacific war was the first protracted conflict that the Japanese had fought on alien soil. In many cases, American and British soldiers captured in battle constituted the first westerners some of the Japanese had ever seen at close quarters.

It has been remarked that the Japanese place great importance on obedience, and this applies not only to the edicts of government but also to social codes. The average Japanese (and Japan is perhaps one of the few countries where the term 'average' can be applied with any meaning) is conditioned by a set code of social responses for given situations. When things happen outside his normal social experience, as they often do in war, the ordinary Japanese soldier and officer had no set response to the situation and he often panicked and behaved savagely because of it. Brutality towards prisoners was an almost inevitable result of the Japanese contact with the West in the war situation, but to describe the Japanese as 'cruel' has no more meaning than to describe any other nation in the same way.

Defeat in war led to occupation, a terrible national trauma for a people who had never before in their history been successfully invaded, but it also led to the first opportunity the Japanese had had to reach a proper appraisal of the westerner. Never before had the West come to Japan in such numbers. With typical adaptability, the Japanese have faced up to the new economic and political challenge of America and western Europe, but it is an open question whether or not they have achieved that 'proper appraisal'.

The modern Japanese is one of the world's greatest tourists as any observer in any capital city will be quick to notice. He is usually recognizable by his expensive camera, ready at the drop of a hat to photograph anyone or anything. The tourist is, however, transient and the Japanese tourist probably gains no more or less from his visits to the West than the tourist of any other nation.

Much more indicative of how well the modern Japanese fits into western society is the Japanese businessman abroad. Apart from those who come to Europe (and to a greater extent the United States) on short business trips, there is now a sizeable number of men who come to European capitals for more extended periods, bringing their families with them. The fact is that many of these families do not fit in well at all, perhaps because they are on limited 'tours of duty' and know that they will be able to return to Japan soon enough. It is interesting to note that, by and large, these families tend to live in the same areas of a city and tend to maintain their own Japanese way of life, as far as this is possible, in a European or American society. The wives, especially, have a difficult time, usually because they do not speak very much of the native language and are left by their husbands to look after the children and manage as best they can.

In general terms, therefore, the Japanese abroad tends not to integrate well, but at the same time he is very anxious to appear integrated to the western way of doing things. Anxiety about loss of face is still a very potent factor in the character of modern Japan, which the westerner, although he has other psychological problems, does not share to the same extent because of the western emphasis on individualism.

Since the war the Japanese have shown a tremendous enthusiasm for study of the West which, by and large, has not been reciprocated. For example, there are about twenty current Japanese journals dealing with English literature, many of them at least semi-popular. The whole of Europe probably could not muster that number on the whole of Japanese civilization, and those that are published are usually for the specialist.

It is perhaps reasonable for a westerner visiting Japan, therefore, to expect the Japanese to have some knowledge of his language at least. Unfortunately, the Japanese share one marked characteristic with the British, a shyness about speaking foreign languages. There are other problems, too, for the visiting westerner. The Japanese, despite their obvious success in the modern world, are, in many respects, still living in the past. One manifestation of this is that throughout Japan, one is showered with *te-miyage* — small presents of nominal value given to visitors. This apparently charming custom, allied to frequently almost excessive courtesy and politeness, is apt to be misleading. Gifts which are given seemingly as a token of goodwill are in fact no more than a kind of gesture used by the donor to ensure a good reception.

In reality, Japanese politeness is no more than a façade which is apt to break down under pressure, and it stems from an obsession with the form rather than the spirit of courtesy. The famous politeness of the Japanese breaks down all too easily, for example, under the stress of the Tokyo rush-hour. In a sense the excessive formality and politeness of the Japanese towards the westerner is a kind of defence mechanism. Because the Japanese identify with a group, they do not want to appear apart from that group which they must necessarily do in dealing with the different types of situation with which a westerner will present them. Naturally, therefore, the best type of response is the formal one which can, in theory, be applied to all situations and accordingly save any possible loss of face.

It is, of course, unreasonable to carp about such things when westerners make so few concessions to Japanese sensibilities. The net result of all this formality, politeness and shyness which the westerner is liable to encounter in his dealings with the Japanese is to make him feel that he is never quite sure where he stands. It constitutes what the westerner usually means if he refers to the Japanese as 'inscrutable'.

The irony of the situation is that the Japanese himself is also equally uncertain. There are certain signs, though, that the Japanese are beginning to take a more positive stand where westerners are concerned even though they understand him no better than he does them. The Olympic Games of 1964, the successful Expo '70 in Osaka, and, most of all, the successful demand for the return of Okinawa by the United States have certainly increased Japanese self-confidence in their quest for a rôle in the modern world.

The next few years will reveal whether this search is transitory, or whether it really does represent a kind of re-assertion of national identity. One thing, however, remains certain — if it is fully to appreciate the character and qualities of one of its potentially most valuable allies, the West generally will have to devote much more time and money to the study of Japan.

A new era *by Richard Storry*

Overwhelmingly, the impression created on the visitor to Japan, from the moment he arrives in Tokyo, is the extreme modernity of the city scene. Coupled with this is a sense of general energy and gusto. What is the origin of all this progress? To find the answer we have to go back at least a hundred years, in fact to 1868 — when the antiquated regime of the Tokugawa Shoguns made way for a new form of government; an historic event known as the Meiji Restoration. In an edict, the 'Charter Oath', drafted by the new government, the youthful Emperor Meiji declared: 'Knowledge shall be sought for all over the world'.

The Meiji Restoration has been interpreted in all sorts of ways by Japanese scholars and commentators. Some have seen it as at least the halfway house on the road to social revolution, because it meant the displacement of feudalism by modern capitalism. Others have seen it as a return to ancient tradition, since in formal terms full political sovereignty was restored to the monarchy after centuries of rule by the warrior class. Yet another version of the Meiji Restoration interprets it as being essentially the product of a struggle for power between opposing groups of *samurai* (warrior) clans.

But what is certain is that the Meiji Restoration meant not only the death of a feudal society, but also a basic change in the Japanese attitude towards the contemporary world. In accordance with the 'Charter Oath' the new government, after 1868, proceeded to adopt all manner of institutions and customs current in the West. The government invited foreigners to Japan as advisers, teachers and technicians of every kind. At the same time, carefully selected young Japanese of ability were sent abroad to learn everything from up-to-date medical practice to the building of steam locomotives and the operation of municipal gasworks. In other words, the Meiji government was the most realistic in Asia (and perhaps in the world).

To the Japanese of the early Meiji era, Great Britain was the very epitome of all that was implied by the term *bummei kaika;* in other words, Civilization and Enlightenment. However, it was not the only model. There was Bismarck's creation, the German Empire, a rising industrial power of striking efficiency in every field. There was the United States. And there was France. From these and other countries Japan adopted and adapted such techniques as she required. 'Knowledge shall be sought for all over the world.' The commandment was taken very seriously.

Thus, if the navy was trained by British officers, the army owed much first to the French and later to the Germans. Silk filature skills were borrowed from Lyons. In Hokkaido, the northern and hitherto largely neglected island, a new provincial capital city, Sapporo, was laid out according to a design prepared by American advisers. Americans, too, heavily influenced the first plans for a modern educational system, to include compulsory primary schooling for all children. British engineers surveyed the routes, and supervised the construction, of the first railways and drove the first locomotives. Medical science and western music were taught in Japan by Germans, while determined and dedicated Japanese travelled to Berlin and Vienna to study these mysteries at their fountainhead.

In a surprisingly short time, the pupil was able to dispense with most of his tutors. In some fields it was found possible to terminate the services of nearly all foreign advisers within a matter of ten years.

I have suggested the reason why Japan's leaders embarked upon headlong modernization. But why were they so successful, on the whole, in carrying it out so rapidly?

Partly the answer is to be found in the nature of Japanese society during the two centuries of feudal seclusion. This society was in many ways extremely rigid, being stratified along class lines that were not easy to cross. Yet at the same time, it was a very secular society. In other words, religion — in the sense of ever-present 'other worldly' concerns and superstitions — did not begin to play in Japan the crucial rôle it filled in a society such as India. Neither Shinto nor Buddhism was unimportant. But the dominant influence was that of Confucianism as adapted to Japanese conditions. The Confucian code is a system of ethics, not a religion in the generally accepted meaning of the term. It is practical and decidedly 'this worldly' — although by no means materialistic. So what is broadly understood by the scientific attitude, with its reliance on cause and effect and on proof dependent on experiment, was not alien, or even unfamiliar, to the educated Japanese of the eighteenth and early nineteenth centuries. Moreover, education in Tokugawa days was not restricted to members of the élite *samurai* class. The children of prosperous farmers and urban merchants commonly attended school. Instruction at school or by private teachers embraced mathematics as well as Chinese classics. A significant minority, perhaps 20 per cent, of the Japanese male population was literate, numerate and remarkably open-minded and intellectually curious by the time Perry's ships appeared in 1853.

It was found, for example, that when the first Japanese official mission travelled across the Pacific to the United States — this was before the Meiji Restoration — the members of the mission, seemingly complete strangers to the modern world, showed no particular surprise when presented with examples of contemporary material technology, such as railways and textile mills. They had seen diagrams and engravings of such machines in Japan and they had quickly mastered the broad principles of their operation.

Rationalism alone, however, would have been insufficient to provide the driving force that propelled Japan into the modern world. The flame of vigour came from the *samurai* ethical code, itself compounded of Confucianism and that strange brand of Buddhism, secular and mystical at the same time, known as Zen. Confucian teaching bound the *samurai* in a web of obligations, the greatest of which was loyalty to his overlord. Zen gave him the inner determination to observe such obligations, in the most single-minded and efficient way. For Zen teaches efficiency above all.

Soon after the Meiji Restoration, the traditional class structure was formally abolished. To drive the lesson home, military service — the cherished privilege of the *samurai* class — became an obligation to which all young males below a certain age, irrespective of social origin, were liable. Equally hard to endure for many warriors was the encouragement they were given to plunge into business and commercial life. But a great deal of propaganda — in articles in the new press and magazines, as well as in books dealing with the western world — was addressed to the *samurai*, and indeed to all Japanese, impressing upon them the argument that there was nothing dishonourable in taking to trade or manufacture. In fact, both Great Britain and the

United States were cited as examples of societies in which the businessman enjoyed and deserved prestige of the highest order.

A proportion of the *samurai* class never adapted itself to the new order of things. These diehards either rose in hopeless revolt or eked out a mere existence in growing penury and distress. But most members of the *samurai* class, inspired by loyalty to the Throne and sustained by the energy and pragmatism derived from their upbringing, threw themselves with a will into the task of helping their country to catch up with the rest of the world. And men who had spent their lives reading the Chinese classics and practising swordsmanship became bankers, ship-chandlers, iron-masters, lumber merchants, stevedores, glass manufacturers, journalists and stockbrokers.

In every case — it is a bold claim to make, but not outrageously so — the motive was almost certainly public-spirited rather than selfish. In other words, personal profit was not consciously thought of as the main incentive. A more cynical view may hold that patriotic duty and the need to make a good living happened to coincide in a very agreeable way. Be that as it may, there is no doubt that the men who were the pioneers of industry and commerce in Japan in the first generation after 1868, tended to come from a *samurai* background, or from families of wealthy farmers, whose ethical code and general manner of life were close to those of the *samurai* class. To this there were some exceptions, of course. The great Mitsui concern grew from the urban trading house of Mitsui, long famous in the feudal period. But in general the old merchant class did not play a prominent rôle in the new Meiji society — possibly because the traditional merchants (unlike most warriors) had too much to lose if they took the risk of entering unfamiliar fields of business.

It was an era in which foreign ideas, through the translation of European books, fascinated the Japanese intelligentsia. So enthusiastic was the interest in the West that some public men actually propounded such outlandish schemes as the total abandonment of the ideographic script, or the wholesale adoption of wheat cultivation instead of rice. Things went so far, in the fashionable worship of western culture, that some reaction was inevitable and was already apparent before the outbreak of war with China in 1894.

Finally, although so much was owed to the West — in terms of ideas, above all, perhaps — the one thing that was not owed by the Japanese was money. The Tokyo government saw the dangers of foreign loans for a country still economically weak, indeed backward. Only two small loans were raised in London in the 1870s. The real cost of industrialization was met from a newly instituted and fairly heavy land tax. This saved Japan from the burden of foreign creditors, at the price of depressing thousands of farmers, creating thereby (until the post-war period) an entirely new class of peasant tenantry in debt to landowners and money-lenders. There was perhaps no other way at that time by which the government could raise the funds it needed. For thanks to treaties signed before 1868, Japan was restricted to a low maximum tariff on imports. Only in the 1890s was the government able to persuade the foreign powers to re-negotiate the 'unequal treaties'.

In retrospect, it is the drive and unity of the age that makes the strongest impression. In the Meiji period, as now, the country seemed to hum like a dynamo. Central, as symbol of progress and focus of intense national love and pride, was the figure of the Emperor Meiji. Even today a certain aura surrounds his name. For his reign lasted until 1912 and it witnessed the transformation of Japan from a rather obscure, feudal, society to one of the great powers of the modern world.

Thus the vigorous, democratic, highly industrialized Japan of today springs from seeds sown a century ago. The harvest of the Meiji Restoration is the high standard of living, the inventiveness and the astonishing productivity of the Japan of the 1970s.

China and Japan *by Arnold Toynbee*

Japan is one of the 'offshore' groups of islands adjoining the Eurasian continent. The intervening stretch of sea is wider than the straits between Indonesia and South-East Asia and between the British Isles and Western Europe. It is therefore not surprising that the Japanese people have a highly distinctive national way of life. The major theme of Japanese history has been the impact of foreign ways of life on the Japanese way, followed by a counter-impact of Japan on the rest of the world.

The foreign impacts on Japan have differed greatly in their age, duration, and intensity. The Chinese impact began at least as early as the sixth century of the Christian Era, and perhaps several centuries before that. In the sixth century the incoming stream of Chinese culture carried with it an Indian element in the shape of Buddhism; but this Indian philosophy or religion had been sinified en route. The western impact on Japan did not begin till the sixteenth century. Japan's counter-impact on the world is little more than a hundred years old. It did not begin till after the Meiji Restoration of 1868.

The Japanese people's reaction to foreign impacts has always been prompt and vigorous. After having adopted Buddhism, in its sinified form in the sixth century, Japan went on to adopt the T'ang dynasty's system of imperial administration in the seventh century. In Japanese hands these loans from China have been modified till, in some cases, their Chinese origin has almost ceased to be recognizable. Yet Chinese culture has entered into the Japanese way of life so deeply that it has become a

permanent ingredient in it. The modern western civilization has overlaid the Chinese in Japan, but its influence is probably more superficial, besides being so much more recent. China's continuing presence is a major factor in Japan's history. It seems likely also to be a major influence on Japan's future.

In its impact on Japan, the West has been much more aggressive and importunate than China. Consequently, Japan has had to be more resourceful and more drastic in the successive steps that she has taken with the object of retaining the initiative in her relations with the West. By comparison with almost all other non-western countries except perhaps Thailand and Russia, she has been very successful in holding her own against the West. Unlike Africa, Southern Asia, and China, she has never allowed herself to fall under western domination, either overt or covert.

After having opened her doors to western penetration rather incautiously in the sixteenth century, Japan deliberately reversed this easy-going policy and retreated into an almost complete self-insulation during the Tokugawa period. The policy of the Tokugawa régime was not only to insulate Japan but to freeze her domestic life. The Tokugawa statesmen realized that insulation would not be possible without domestic unification and stabilization. The two sides of their policy were interdependent, but on both its sides the policy eventually broke down.

Perhaps Japan could have kept the West at arm's length with western armaments of the seventeenth-century style if the West itself had remained technologically stagnant. But in the eighteenth century the Industrial Revolution took place in the West, and nineteenth-century western weapons were powerful enough to batter down Japan's closed doors, as Commodore Perry demonstrated pacifically but cogently in 1853. Moreover, it was just as impossible for the *bakufu* (feudal government) to arrest domestic economic and social change as it was for it to prevent the West from forging ahead in technology. The *bakufu* did effectively tame the *daimyo* (feudal lords); but the price of this domestic political feat was the transfer of wealth from the *daimyo's* hands — and from the *bakufu's* own hands, too — into the hands of a new class of businessmen, some of whom organized themselves in large-scale corporations. The *bakufu* had neither intended nor foreseen a pacific domestic revolution, but, in the event, this turned out fortunately for Japan. By the time nineteenth-century western artillery had made it impracticable for Japan to maintain her policy of self-insulation, Japanese businessmen had equipped themselves for competing with Westerners on equal terms in the fields of western commerce and industry — fields that Japan now needed to enter in order to provide herself with the 'sinews of war' of a modern western degree of potency.

By the time of the Meiji Restoration, four centuries of western maritime expansion and scientific and technological progress had knit together the whole surface of the globe for the first time in mankind's history. The globe had now been unified as a military arena and as a market, without yet having been unified either culturally or politically. Japan, stepping out into this dangerous semi-unified world, has made a dynamic counter-impact on it. This counter-impact has been both military and economic, and, in both activities, Japan has experienced dramatic alternations of successes and reverses.

In war, Japan has won a series of victories, beginning with her defeat of China in 1894 and culminating in 1941 in her destruction of the American fleet in Pearl Harbour and her conquest of the British, Dutch, and French colonial possessions in South-East Asia. This series of military adventures ended in the biggest disaster that Japan has ever incurred so far. In 1945, for the first time in her history, Japan was occupied militarily by a foreign conqueror, and she lost the whole of the empire that she had been building up in the course of the preceding half-century. But, since 1945,

Japan has compensated for this military disaster by achieving an economic triumph. She has made herself into the second or third greatest economic power in the world, outstripping Western Germany, an ally of Japan's in the Second World War who has been spurred by a still more crushing military defeat to make comparable post-war economic exertions. The 'co-prosperity sphere' and the 'Lebensraum' that eluded Japan's and Germany's grasp when these economic goals were sought by means of military conquest have been achieved, as aftermaths of military defeat, by peaceful economic penetration. Whatever future mankind may have in store, it is certain that Japan will continue to play a leading part in the world's life.

Japan's post-war economic success has been the reward of the Japanese people's own enterprise and energy; but an enabling condition for it has been the policy of the United States. The Administration at Washington has held a 'nuclear umbrella' over Japan's head and has allowed the United States to be a market for Japanese manufacturers; and it is thanks to this American policy that Japan, since 1945, has been able to spend a minimum of her resources on armaments and to concentrate on economic productivity in the non-military field. But this condition enabling Japan's economic boom was called in question in 1971 by two abrupt new departures in American policy. Washington imposed a 10 per cent surcharge on imports into the United States, pending a re-alignment of exchange rates and a reform of the whole of the international monetary system. President Nixon also arranged to visit Peking and proclaimed his intention of bringing about a détente between the United States and Continental China.

These two American actions, taken together, have raised the question of Japan's future relations with China. Right down to the Meiji Restoration, China was, for Japan, still 'the Middle Kingdom' — not in the political terms of being Japan's suzerain, but in the sense of being the fountain-head of Japanese culture. The Tokugawa *bakufu* favoured neo-Confucianism, especially in its most recent form, as it had been presented by Wang Yang-ming. However, before Commodore Perry's first uninvited appearance in Yedo Bay, the Japanese had already taken note of the potency of nineteenth-century western armaments. They had seen remote and tiny Britain win an almost effortless victory over China in the Opium War of 1839-42; and this observation, followed up by China's defeat in her more stubbornly contested war of 1858-60 with Britain and France, was one of the experiences that led Japan to reverse the Tokugawa policy of self-insulation. Japan now acted swiftly to make herself a match for the West militarily according to the nineteenth-century standard of western weapons. She also made the social and economic changes in her domestic life that were the conditions necessary for equipping herself with nineteenth-century western armaments. When the Japanese saw the Chinese hesitating and bungling, in spite of a humiliating defeat which ought to have stimulated the Chinese to do what was being done by Japan without this brutal stimulus, the age-old Japanese veneration for China was temporarily shattered.

The Japanese now succumbed to the temptation of seeing the Chinese, through modern western eyes, as 'natives' who were to be despised and exploited. From 1894 to 1945, the Japanese emulated and even surpassed the westerners and the Russians in their ill-treatment of China. But Japan's experience in her relations with China from 1931 to 1945 has led (at least, this is my impression) to another revulsion in the Japanese attitude towards China. By 1945, Japan was prostrate, while China was still on her feet. Once again, as so often before in the long course of Chinese history, China has displayed her characteristic staying-power — this time at Japan's expense. The awe Japan had felt for China until 1868 has revived since 1945. Since then, there has been a feeling in Japan that, after all, Japan's future may lie in her relations with

China. President Nixon's action raised this question of future Sino-Japanese relations in an urgent practical way. Japan's market in the United States has proved to be precarious, and China has taken the first steps towards becoming a nuclear power. In the long run, may not China be going to count for more than the United States in the determination of Japan's destiny?

Since 1949, the United States has put pressure on Japan to follow the American lead in cold-shouldering Continental China. This has been part of the price of America's favours to Japan. Now that American policy towards Continental China has suddenly veered round, it would be natural for Japan to abandon an anti-Chinese policy which she has pursued only out of deference to American wishes. Is a lasting rapprochement between Japan and China a practical possibility? The answer to this question depends on the strength of China's resentment towards Japan and on the extent of Japan's power to disarm China's hostility.

Chinese hostility towards Japan has been inevitable. Japan's Western-like and Russian-like treatment of China during the half-century 1894-1945 must have been resented by the Chinese even more than the misdeeds of the western and the Russian barbarians. The barbarians were aliens; the Japanese were old converts to the Chinese tradition of culture. It must have been particularly galling for the Chinese to have been treated barbarously by their Japanese cultural kith and kin. Chinese suspicions of Japan's future intentions towards China must also have been re-awakened by the post-war anti-Chinese stance that Japan has adopted under American pressure. In these unpropitious circumstances, a rapprochement between Japan and China might have been a forlorn hope, if Japan did not hold a trump card that America has fortunately thrust into her hand.

After the Second World War, the Americans not only disarmed Japan; they prevailed on the Japanese to write into Japan's new constitution an article in which Japan pledges herself never to re-arm and never again to go to war. This article in the Japanese constitution seems to me to be the key to Japan's future relations with China and consequently to be also the key to Japan's own destiny. If any Japanese action can disarm Chinese suspicions, this will be it.

If Japan and China were to succeed in forming a mutually trustful partnership with each other, their combined economic and cultural power would confer on them the political power to swing the world. They could swing it towards the stable peace that is one of the world's crying needs, and they could then perhaps work out, for themselves and for the rest of the world, a tolerable version of the modern western way of life that has been carrying mechanization and urbanization to intolerable lengths.

The Japanese people are acutely aware of the present-day evils of pollution and congestion. They have paid for their post-war economic boom by bringing these evils on themselves in a more than western degree. Yet Japan possesses, in her own distinctive way of life, a tradition of seeking to establish a harmony between man and the non-human remainder of Nature. This, if I am not mistaken, is the spirit of Shinto; and 'live and let live' is the spirit of Buddhism, the Indian philosophy that is so deeply ingrained in both the Japanese and the Chinese traditions. Together, Japan and China might perhaps succeed in solving for mankind the problems that have been created by the world-wide diffusion of the modern western way of life.

A very particular Englishman

by Richard Storry

On 19 April, 1600, there appeared off the town of Funai (the modern Oita), on the Kyushu coast of Japan, a Dutch vessel, the first ever seen in those parts. She was the *Liefde* (Charity), of Rotterdam. When the local inhabitants rowed out to her they encountered a horrifying spectacle. The *Liefde* was manned by six human scarecrows barely able to stand upright. In an even more pitiful condition were twelve seamen so weak from starvation they could move across the deck only on their hands and knees. These eighteen men were all that remained of a ship's company of 110 that had set sail from Holland nearly two years earlier. The Japanese took the survivors ashore, installing them in a house where they were well cared for. Nevertheless, for some of them rescue had come too late. Six died within days. The others recovered.

Japan was governed at this time by a small council of great lords, of whom the most powerful was Tokugawa Ieyasu, soon to consolidate the position of himself and his descendants by a famous victory over his rivals at the battle of Sekigahara. When news of the *Liefde* reached him Ieyasu was at Osaka, and he sent orders for the ship's captain to be sent to him without delay. But the captain, Jacob Quaeckernack, was still too weak to travel. The next in seniority happened to be an Englishman, Will Adams, a master mariner and pilot of the *Liefde*. Being in better shape than Quaeckernack, he took the latter's place and was conveyed by ship up the Inland Sea to Osaka, arriving there on 12 May, 1600, and soon afterwards he was brought into the presence of Ieyasu.

Many years later, in a letter to his wife in England, Adams described this first encounter with Ieyasu:

'Coming before the King (Ieyasu), he viewed me well, and seemed to be wonderful favourable. He made many signs unto me, some of which I understood, and some I did not. In the end there came one that could speak Portuguese. By him the King demanded of me what land I was, and what moved us to come to his land, being so far off.'*

It was fortunate for Will Adams and his shipmates that Ieyasu, justly regarded as one of the greatest figures in Japanese history, was endowed with uncommon shrewdness and independence of mind. A lesser man in Ieyasu's position might have been swayed by the accusations made by certain Portuguese Jesuits in Japan, who had hastened to spread abroad their conviction that the *Liefde* survivors, being Protestant heretics, were no more than robbers and pirates. Ieyasu, however, clearly found Adams an interesting and likeable stranger. There was to develop between them a relationship of mutual respect and genuine friendship.

Who was this Englishman who would succeed in making for himself a new and prosperous life in the utterly strange surroundings of seventeenth-century Japan? Will Adams was an exact contemporary of Shakespeare's being born in the same year, 1564. His birthplace was Gillingham in Kent. In boyhood he served a long apprenticeship with a shipbuilder in London and then became a skilled mariner, a master pilot, sailing in both English and Dutch vessels on several ambitious voyages, as far as West Africa in one direction and Spitzbergen in the other. He married an English girl in 1589; they had one child, a daughter christened Deliverance. Nine years later he joined

*P. G. Rogers: *The First Englishman in Japan* (London, The Harvill Press, 1956) p. 27

Plate 3: *Page from the log-book of Will Adams. Reproduced by courtesy of the Bodleian Library, Oxford.*

Plate 4: *Japanese artist's impression of a Dutch merchant with his servants*

2

the 20 daye being frydey we went about our lighter to
trim our ship but our lyme was bad that wee could do not...
were fayne to tary till other weder... this
this day fayre weder the wind at n E

4

the 21 being saterdaye ther cam a noble man to let over our
... from the road in o Naba his name was ... this daye
I hard that the Emperor had gott the victory of the ...
was glad to hear this day we went about to mak a ...
and other lighters in triming our ... this day ...
... this day very fayre wether the wind ...

the 22 being ... day we went about our lighters in
triming our ship this day fayre weder the wind
at S W t w S w

5   the 23 being monday we still went about to trim
our ship the wind ... foule weder

6   the 24 being tewesdaye we still did Calle... in
and ... out this day we set Carpenters a work to mak
pompes this day it was very ... weder but the wind ...
all ...

the 25 ... in our ship the Carpenters work was don
... out bond were nere don this daye the
7   ... did hinder our work the wind was no ray... weder
being wednesdaye

8   the 26 daye we began to tak in ballast and still Callking
... in ... out but at noone we ... not Cover...
... it woorke but would have ther hyre ... was ...
... in ground ... had much ado ... this
day ... this day the wind at n n w...
weder ...

9   the 27 daye the boteswaine cam to me in the Cappestio
of the Company for ther other ... wayes I told them it was
not due to them before they came to Sian at ... I ...
... Sian ... I would pay them and after I would not woold not
... but yf they had anyght don... I would mak them ...
... but yf they had be apoynted by the Justis of Joppan and
... I should be apoynted by the Justis of Joppan
... wee... to ... them I would give them a bill of my
... ther ... but they would not stand to the Justis of Joppan
... But would have ther demand or me to forward in the
... but returned

HOLLA

フランス
拂郎察

an important and novel Dutch venture — five ships bound for the Far East by way of Cape Horn and the Pacific — together with his brother and two English friends. The fleet was unable to stay together after rounding the Horn. Only the *Liefde*, desperately short of food, reached harbour in Japan; and of the Englishmen only Adams survived.

Will Adams, 36 years of age when he was taken before Ieyasu, had picked up Portuguese in the course of his travels. This was the only foreign tongue, apart from Chinese, that the Japanese could speak at that time. Knowledge of Portuguese meant that early communication between Adams and Ieyasu was not excessively difficult; and the latter was soon able to judge Adams's native ability and range of knowledge. Here Adams possessed a valuable qualification. In addition to being a skilled pilot he knew how to build ships, thanks to his London apprenticeship. And Ieyasu commanded him to design a western rigged vessel. Adams was reluctant to undertake the task, disclaiming any particular skill; but he was in no position to refuse. So at Ito, in the Izu peninsula, he supervised the construction of an 80-ton ship, which proved to be seaworthy; this enhanced his reputation in the eyes of Ieyasu and the Japanese authorities. After that Ieyasu sent for Adams on many occasions, employing him as an interpreter in dealing with Europeans and as a consultant on such matters as mathematics, European state affairs, navigation and maritime lore generally.

Ieyasu had become *shogun* in 1603 and he established Yedo (the modern Tokyo) as the headquarters of his government. It was there, or at his castle at Shizuoka, that Ieyasu received the Englishman, treating him with great kindness and clearly placing much confidence in his advice. In only one matter did Ieyasu oppose Adams's own declared wish: he would not allow the Englishman to return to his home in Kent. But this prohibition was not maintained for more than a few years. The fact is that although Adams was often homesick and indeed never forgot his wife and daughter in England life in Japan was made very comfortable for him.

Ieyasu gave Adams the status of a minor Tokugawa vassal, together with a country estate on the Miura peninsula close to Yedo; and here Adams was granted complete authority over some ninety retainers. He had a position in Japan that few, if any, Europeans have enjoyed.

In his own country, it must be stressed, Will Adams, as an experienced master mariner, commanded a great deal of respect. Ocean navigation was a relatively new and expanding science and Adams's prestige in the English society of his day was high. In Japan, however, Adams was a nobleman — a rank he could not have attained in England unless he ventured on the dangerous road to riches and fame as a free-booting sea captain, like Hawkins, trading in African slaves and harassing Spanish galleons.

Pragmatic and businesslike, Adams did not allow religious or national predilections to stand in the way when it came to rendering services to Portuguese and Spanish traders in Japan. And he was soon prosperous enough to buy a house in the Nihonbashi district of Yedo, a transaction commemorated in later years by the name of a city block, Anjim-cho ('Pilot' street), which still survives in Tokyo. Moreover, he married a Japanese girl, who was to bear him a son and daughter (Joseph and Susanna). It seems to have been a satisfactory and happy marriage — although it is perhaps worth noting that Adams was father of a third child in Japan, by a Japanese woman of Hirado, the Kyushu port where the Dutch and English established trading posts in the early years of the seventeenth century.

The commercial ventures of the Dutch and English, however, were slower to materialize than Adams had hoped. It was not until 1611 that the Dutch trading station of Hirado was fully established. And it was in the same year that the English East India Company despatched three ships under command of Captain John Saris for the Far East. Saris was instructed by the company to pay particular attention, on arrival in

Plate 5: *A Frenchman and his wife. From a book published in Japan about 1850 describing customs, geography and government of the outside world*

23

Japan, to the advice of Will Adams, whom the company understood to be 'in great favour with the King' (Ieyasu). Furthermore, Saris was told to provide a cabin for Adams, should the latter wish to return to England to visit his family.

It has often been said that the East India Company made a fatal blunder in not taking the sound advice given by Adams, that their trading post should be at Urago on Yedo Bay, rather than in a Kyushu town such as Hirado, remote from the *shogun's* capital. At least one important reason why, in the event, Hirado, not Uraga, was chosen lay in the dislike that Saris and Adams came to have for each other. The account of their meeting makes it clear that Saris and at least some of the English merchants formed a bad impression of Will Adams. They thought him conceited; and they were shocked to discover that he was engaged in business with Portuguese and Spanish merchants as well as with the Dutch. It is always irritating, even for the mildest of men, while in a foreign land, to be at the mercy of a compatriot who speaks the language of that country, is familiar with its customs, and so monopolizes the functions of an interpreter. No doubt, too, Saris — a man of better formal education than Adams — felt almost personally insulted by the necessity of having to maintain a courteous front towards a man whom he regarded as his social inferior. Snobbery, in other words, was not missing from this equation.

But such feelings had to be held in check; and it must be said that Adams gave invaluable help to Saris, accompanying him to audiences with both Ieyasu and his son, Hidetada, and using his own influence with Ieyasu to secure a written grant of trading privileges for the London East India Company. Adams also accommodated Saris and other Englishmen from the *Clove* on his country estate for three days, while the party inspected the harbour of Uraga close by.

It seems likely that Saris had made up his mind before his visit to Yedo that Hirado, not Uraga, was the best place for a permanent trading post (to the disappointment of Adams). The decision made, he prepared to set off in the *Clove* on the journey home, having spent the best part of six months in Japan.

Adams could have returned to England in the *Clove* and at one time seemed ready to do so. But he changed his mind, telling Saris that he wanted to remain longer in Japan, in order to improve his financial position. The real reason, undoubtedly, was his dislike of Saris, who (as Adams put it in a letter to the East India Company) had done him 'divers injuries'. Before he sailed, Saris concluded a contract with Adams, after a good deal of haggling, whereby Adams became an employee of the East India Company for the next two years. Saris also left behind him with the little community of English merchants at Hirado a 'Remembrance', or general guide, and this included several derogatory remarks about Adams and the warning that he was not to be trusted with the company's money.

But Richard Cocks, in charge at Hirado as 'Captain of the English' (as the Japanese called him), came to esteem Adams, although he continued to disapprove of the latter's friendly association with Dutchmen and other foreigners. It was Saris who was to suffer a loss of face in the regard of his employers. On return to England it was discovered that he had been trading in goods on his own account. Furthermore, the company's agents unearthed in his cabin a collection of pornographic picture books acquired in Japan. On the orders of the East India Company these were publicly burnt.

A year after Saris had left, Richard Cocks entrusted Adams with command of a ship bought from the Japanese and fitted out, under the supervision of Adams, for a voyage to Siam. The vessel carried a crew of about sixty. Travelling as passengers were two English merchants from Hirado and several Japanese merchants hoping for trade with the Siamese. Bad fortune attended this venture. Storm damage forced the ship to put in for repairs at Okinawa; and the crew was mutinous. The voyage to Siam was abandoned. The ship returned to Japan. It is said that the sweet potatoes from Okinawa in her cargo — planted by Cocks in his garden at Hirado — were the first to be grown in Japan.

Six months later, early in December 1615, Adams took the same ship on a successful voyage to Siam, returning to Hirado in July 1616. The venture showed a handsome profit for the East India Company.

While Adams was at sea his exalted protector and benefactor, Ieyasu, died, in June 1616. This marked the end of Adams's unchallenged influence at court in Yedo. Ieyasu's son, Hidetada, appears to have had no particular affection for Adams. Indeed, Hidetada, as *shogun*, showed himself to be increasingly suspicious of Europeans, notably those of the Catholic faith.

In September 1619 Adams fell ill. The illness, whatever it was, proved fatal. Adams died on 16 May, 1620, in his fifty-seventh year, in or near Hirado, since an inventory of his possessions was drawn up there on 22 May.

In the suburbs of Yokosuka, at Hemi where Adams had his estate, stand tombs alleged to be those of Adams and his Japanese wife. Mrs Adams, who died four years after her husband, is known to have been buried at Hemi. But the probability is that Adams was interred at Hirado. He left a lengthy will, which did not neglect to make provision for his wife and daughter in England. Indeed, Adams had arranged for regular payments to be made to his English wife, through the East India Company, for several years before his death. In his will he was careful to provide a sum exclusively for his daughter, Deliverance, in case his wife should remarry and (as Richard Cocks put it) 'carry all from his child'. Adams's son Joseph was confirmed by the *shogun* in possession of the Hemi estate. It is known that Joseph had been trained as a pilot; and he made a number of voyages to south-east Asia before Japan became a 'closed country' in 1637. Thereafter the progeny of Will Adams in Japan and in England are lost to historical record.

But the memory of Adams, or *Miura Anjin* (as he was known in Japanese), is kept alive by an annual festival held in his honour at Ito in the Izu Peninsula, where he built the ship for Ieyasu. From time to time, also, commemorative celebrations are held at Hemi, in the Yokosuka suburbs.

There seems to be no portrait of Adams. But during his voyages south from Hirado he kept a log, a daily chronicle of events; and this is one of the treasures of the Bodleian Library, Oxford. From this, from letters he wrote, and from the Diary of Richard Cocks, it is not difficult to form at least a rough assessment of the character and personality of Will Adams. He was clearly resourceful, utterly reliable and determined, with a good business head on his shoulders. These qualities of themselves, however, would not have been enough to impress Ieyasu so strongly in Adams's favour. It is evident that he also had a sound knowledge of the general political situation between the states of Europe. Indeed, one might go so far as to call Adams a typical Elizabethan, in his mixture of shrewdness, robust energy and freedom from narrow prejudice.

France and Japan *by Jean-Pierre Lehmann*

Although France did enjoy a position of prominence among Japan's new western tutors for a very brief period in the late nineteenth century, she was soon overshadowed by Britain, Germany and the United States. France had signed her treaty of friendship and commerce with Japan in 1858 which was followed, two years later, by the arrival of her first diplomatic representative, Duchesne de Bellecourt. Succeeding him came one of the *bêtes noires* of Japanese diplomatic historians, Léon Roches. Roches was an extremely energetic man and although some of his activities in Japan were rather questionable, he stands out as a friend of Japan and of the Japanese. Roches failed in his enterprise in that he backed the wrong cause at the wrong time; as the shogunal government was tottering to its fall, Roches thought he discerned a strong desire for reform and a spirit of renovation in the person of the last Tokugawa shogun, Hitotsubashi. In order to help him to this end, Roches had a military mission sent from France to train Japanese officers; had the arsenal at Yokosuka built under French auspices and sold arms to the shogunal government to meet the difficulties it was facing with the southern Choshu fief. Roches arranged to have the Shogun's younger brother go on study leave to Paris under the good care and wise tutelage of Napoleon III and also encouraged Japan to be represented at the Paris Expo of 1867 — the first time Japanese works of art officially figured at an international exhibition in Europe. The latter enterprise was not, however, a complete diplomatic success due to another Frenchman, Comte de Montblanc, having succeeded in presenting works from Satsuma, one of the two main rival fiefs.

For nearly two years French influence in practically every field — diplomacy, military affairs and politics — was at its apex. The failure of the Shogunate to withstand the winds of change and the growing national discontent led by the combined forces of the southern fiefs heralded the end of prominent French influence, having been so closely allied to the shogunal cause, and although France did continue to play a rôle in Japan's modernization it was a small one compared to the other three western nations mentioned earlier.

Yet despite this relative paucity of contact, or perhaps because of it, there exists on both sides a mutual fascination. Fosco Maraini in his *Meeting With Japan* compares the relations between the various western nations and Japan and concludes that '. . . French and Japanese approach each other with the fewest mental reservations, the most open mutual humanity; that is why they achieve understanding.' One reason may well be that apart from this short period of French prominence mentioned above and the French 'stab in the back of Japan' in 1895 (when France joined Russia and Germany in the Triple Intervention forcing Japan to relinquish the Liaotung peninsula after her victory in the Sino-Japanese war), France and Japan have not had that many reasons for serious mis-understandings. Thus by and large the literary, artistic and intellectual meeting of French and Japanese minds has not been marred by complicated political, military, or economic entanglements.

What evidence is there of this mutual fascination today? It is almost everywhere and at almost every level. The French tourist in Tokyo will find a bar near Roppongi called *Chambord* and may well wonder whether the name refers to the château in the Loire or the elusive Duc de Chambord, alias Henri V. There are countless other cafés and bars with French names from Pierre (where one can eat *éclairs, profiterolles* and even a *Napoléon*) to Place Vendôme. The Japanese have incorporated French words into their own language, as they have with other western languages; for instance, the post-war period is called *apure* (from après guerre), but in this day of leisure possibly the most popular is *vacansu.*

French *Haute couture* has had a tremendous success in Japan; on one occasion while taking a train from Matsushima to Sendai a Japanese student, upon hearing that I was French, asked me if, of all Frenchmen, I knew Pierre Cardin! French *cuisine* is well known and well appreciated (there is a Maxim's in the basement of the Sony Building in Tokyo) and since the 1860s the Japanese have shown a marked affinity for French wines and no doubt *dégustation de vins* may soon enter the Japanese language as well. French music is equally popular from the classical to the *chansons (Un Gamin de Paris, Les Feuilles Mortes,* etc ...) sung by French and Japanese alike and constantly heard on the radio. Exhibitions of French paintings draw massive crowds. Sartre and Simone de Beauvoir spoke to packed audiences a few years ago, and when I was teaching in a university in Tokyo I often had to admit to my students that I was much less erudite than they were in French literature (prominent authors being Anatole France, Romain Rolland and Zola), even though these students were studying economics, history and political science and not French literature. In the 1950s Brigitte Bardot had a considerable impact and not a few young Japanese girls adopted the Bardot hairstyle. Similarly, and on a deeper level, the French films of the *Nouvelle Vague* had their impact, in particular Louis Malle's *Les Amants,* which showed to the still comparatively secluded young Japanese (compared that is to today when so many Japanese travel all around Europe) that in the West there was a mode of thought other than John Wayne's, even though one slightly shocked lady was overheard complaining that there were 'too many *cocus* (cuckolds)'.

Another personal recollection brings me to Paris this time, when on that very beautiful sunny Easter Sunday of 1969 my wife and I ventured to Montmartre, where neither of us had been for many years, and were amazed to find such a large number of Japanese artists. We were amazed, but less so than the two coach loads of Japanese businessmen, all neatly dressed in dark suits, well groomed, beholding their long-haired, bearded, red-shirted, blue-jeaned, sandalled compatriots. Paris as a sort of mecca of Japanese artists has a long tradition; the most famous product of this pilgrimage being Leonard Fujita, but there are countless others. An exhibition of the Japanese painters having studied in Paris in the 1920s at the Ohara museum of Kurashiki in the early 1970s was most rewarding; the works of artists such as Hayashi Takeshi, Nakagawa Kazumasa, Umehara Ryuaburo, Sakamoto Hanjiro (in particular his 'Yellow Horse'), Koga Harue, Maeta Kanji (especially his remarkably gripping 'Two Labourers'), Koide Narashige (with his very sensual 'Nude on Chinese Bed') and others disproving Kipling by showing how harmoniously East and West can meet.

The attraction France has for the Japanese artistic tradition is of long and fruitful standing. Again, however, this facet of Franco-Japanese relations has been by no means a one-way traffic. There was a time in the second half of the nineteenth century when 'things Japanese' were the rage in Paris, the fashion known as *Japonisme*. Various artists or literary men — Théophile Gautier, the Goncourt Brothers and others — claimed to be the instigators of this fashion. One authority of this period, Earl Miner, suggests as a beginning the discovery by Félix Bracquemond of a volume of Hokusai's *Manga* in 1856 (two years before the first Franco-Japanese treaty). Be that as it may, there is no doubt that the discovery of the Japanese colour wood-block print had one of the deepest influences in the history of French art, for it gave birth to the school of Impressionism. This was far from an unconscious influence. Not one of the Impressionists ever failed to acknowledge and praise the artistic quality, the genius, the spontaneity, of the Japanese prints. As will be seen in a moment, this *crise de Japonisme* affected writers as much as painters, and the juxtaposition of the two can probably best be seen in Manet's painting of Zola at his desk surrounded by *japonaiseries*.

French writers of the period were not so much influenced by Japanese literature, although later poets such as Paul-Louis Couchoud, Gilbert de Voisins, Julien Vocance and others will attempt to write *haiku,* inspired by the poetry of Bassho, as they were by Japanese art and curios. The appeal of the exotic, of the delicate, dreams of gardens, lotus flowers, tea-houses, *geisha* and even the virile bravado of the *samurai* inspired many a French work. Especially to be noted are those of Théophile Gautier's daughter, Judith, with titles such as *La Marchande de Sourires, Princesses d'Amour, Fleurs d'Orient,* etc, as well as the poems of José-Maria de Hérédia and many others. These were the writings of the group calling themselves the *Parnassiens* and in constant communion with *japonaiseries*. One of the hostesses of a *salon* catering to the *Parnassiens*, Nina de Villard, apparently went so far in her *Japonisme* as to receive her guests dressed in a *kimono*.

Not only in painting and writing, but also in music was *Japonisme* reflected, for instance in the operetta, *La Princesse Jaune,* composed by Camille Saint-Saëns. Even the statesman Clemenceau, partly due to his association with the *Parnassiens* and partly, no doubt, due to his friendship with the Japanese statesman, Saionji Kimmochi, while the latter resided in France as a student and whom Clemenceau was to meet later in slightly different circumstances both being their respective countries' principal delegates at the Peace Conference of Versailles, was not immune to *Japonisme*, for not only did he decorate his house with many Japanese works of art and curios, but he even wrote a play with a Japanese theme, *Le Voile du Bonheur.*

These impressions of Japan and the Japanese way of life by people who had never set foot in Japan were often erroneous enough, but they were certainly not malicious or slanderous in any way. Japan was depicted as a country of dreams, of fascination, of beautiful, delicate women and fearless men, a country of wisdom and infinite aesthetic sense. Perhaps the blow that heralded the beginning of the end of *Japonisme* as a fad was the publication of Pierre Loti's *Madame Chrysanthème* in 1888. Loti went to Japan but did not like what he saw and in his book portrays the Japanese as devious and ridiculous. This work is practically the only one in French to have displayed the Japanese in such an unfavourable light; but the unfortunate thing about it was that Loti was very widely read. One scholar, William Schwartz, maintains that Loti's book was read by the Czar and influenced him and his entourage to believe that they had nothing to fear from the Japanese — a mistake they would realize too late after their defeat in the war of 1904-5. This Japanese victory over France's ally and the increasing contact of Frenchmen and Japanese (and the tremendous success of the Japanese pavilion at the Paris Exhibition of 1900) finally dispelled the influences of Loti, and the publication of Anatole France's *Sur la Pierre Blanche* even before the end of the war, and Paul Valéry's *Yalou,* returned to French readers the favourable image of the

Japanese they were accustomed to, not to mention in later years the works of Paul Claudel, one-time French ambassador to Tokyo.

France's reaction to Japan today still gives evidence of this mutual fascination. The number of antique shops all over the country carrying Japanese works of art and curios is amazing. In the artistic field Alain Resnais' *Hiroshima Mon Amour*, comes to mind and in my opinion is the only western film that deals interestingly with a Japanese subject. French knowledge of Japanese literature is limited, however, and this is due principally to the very few Japanese-speaking Frenchmen the country has at its disposal, hence a paucity of translated works.

The French artistic influence on Japan is not one-sided, and neither is the Japanese influence on French men of letters. French literature had both a purely literary influence and a political influence. It is said that when the leader of the so-called movement for freedom and popular rights, Itagaki Taisuke, travelled to France he met Victor Hugo and asked him how the political conscience of the Japanese could be aroused; Victor Hugo suggested they read political novels, Itagaki asked him which ones and Hugo quite simply answered 'mine'; whereupon Itagaki returned to Japan laden with the works of Hugo. These were translated and later on imitated by Kitamura Tokoku who at one time wanted to be the 'Hugo of Japan'. Of course by this time Japanese readers were fairly well acquainted with the works of French writers, but of an earlier period, when the thoughts of French political philosophers, especially Jean-Jacques Rousseau, were as much a fad among the intense followers of the *jiyuminkenundo* as *Japonisme* was the fad with the *Parnassiens*, Japan at the time had an expert of world standing on Jean-Jacques Rousseau in the person of Nakae Chomin. After the liberal political movement was dispelled in the 1880s, French influence was more a peripheral one appealing to a literary élite in the twentieth century, especially among the so-called Naturalist School of Japanese writers, in particular Mori Ogai, Shimazaki Toson and Ozaki Koyo, all especially interested in Zola.

Much more could be said on the meeting of French and Japanese minds, and perhaps this brief review will have given some indication of the extent to which it existed and perhaps explain to a degree why it is that this mutual fascination has existed now for over a century.

The long voyage to Japan

by Michael Cooper

One of the most fascinating items of Japanese art are the so-called *nanban byōbu*, or Southern Barbarian screens, painted by Japanese artists at the beginning of the seventeenth century. About sixty of these folding screens are still extant, and they depict the arrival of the European traders (or Southern Barbarians) at the port of Nagasaki, on the island of Kyushu. In the long and varied history of Japanese painting, more subtle and delicate works of art have doubtlessly been produced, yet these large golden screens, crammed with colourful detail and portraying the arriving Europeans as tall, long-nosed men dressed in splendid costumes, are full of absorbing interest.

Most of the screens illustrate the Portuguese vessel, known as a carrack, or *nao*, which with its three or four decks and displacement up to 1,500 tons was the largest ship afloat in those days. The vessel is shown anchored off Nagasaki, its flags bravely flying, crew members performing dizzy acrobatic feats in the rigging, and the captain-major, or *capitão-mor*, issuing orders on deck. Yet it is well to bear in mind that these screens were produced for decorative purposes, intended to embellish the luxurious Japanese palaces and mansions being built at that time. So while the artists portray the ship, its crew and passengers with considerable accuracy, they understandably allowed themselves some licence when it came to depicting the actual state of the *nao* as it entered port. For with distressing frequency the annual carrack would limp into Nagasaki in a woeful condition, its sails shredded, mast cracked, cargo jettisoned and passengers sick. But such a scene, of course, would hardly make a suitable decoration for a Japanese nobleman's mansion, and so the *nanban byōbu* invariably show a smart ship with hearty sailors busily off-loading the valuable cargo of Chinese silk.

It is difficult, if not impossible, for us to appreciate fully the dangers and hardships involved in the long voyage from Europe to Japan in the sixteenth and seventeenth centuries. Today one can catch a plane in London and arrive in Tokyo on the following day, the journey accomplished with comfort and safety. But in the time of the Southern Barbarians, the voyage took a minimum of two years to complete and often entailed a nightmare of hardship, privation and danger.

In the first place, the voyage took place only once a year; if the traveller happened to arrive a little late in Lisbon and missed the ship's departure, he would have to wait twelve months for the next scheduled trip. For it was only in late spring that suitable winds blew and enabled the clumsy ships to sail southwards. But even if the *nao* started punctually in March, there was no guarantee that the weather would cooperate. Thus, the Portuguese fleet for the 1574 Indies' voyage set sail punctually on 10 March, only to return back to Lisbon a week or so later because of contrary winds.

Worse still, a ship could be stranded in a calm on or near the Equator and idle in the torrid heat for several weeks until a breeze sprang up again. Passing the Cape of Good Hope was literally a hit-or-miss affair. The art of navigation was still undeveloped, and although pilots could calculate their north-south latitude fairly accurately, they had no means of determining their precise longitude. Recourse was had to scanning the sky for birds, or peering down into the sea to note any change in the colour of the water. These somewhat elementary indications certainly helped the sailors to know that land was near, but they left a good deal to be desired when dangerous shoals and rocks were to be avoided. One mistaken turn of the helm and more than a thousand lives could be endangered.

For the great carracks were packed, often grossly overpacked, with merchandise and passengers. Every available space, however small, was utilized to cram more cargo aboard. What little room was left was allotted to the passengers and crew, and some of the larger ships carried as many as 1,200 men in their confined space.

Who were the people that undertook this perilous, protracted voyage? Basically there were three types of traveller. First, of course, there was the crew — perhaps as many as 150-200 manning each ship. Some of them would be young boys in their early teens, mostly Portuguese. From Goa onwards, however, there would be a good proportion of Asians. Many of the crew would be completely unlettered and inexperienced in their duties (on one ship the captain hung up onions on one side and leeks on the other to show the difference between port and starboard); some were sometimes press-ganged into service. Secondly, there were the general passengers, largely merchants and soldiers — the latter having been recruited or press-ganged to man the garrisons in Goa, Malacca and elsewhere. Obviously, a desperate lot of men and mainly Portuguese. 'Merchants,' so called, could be anybody from men of culture to penniless boys running away to find their fortune (more often their death) in the Indies. At times, they were said to have travelled with 'only a water container and a pot of marmalade' (but why marmalade?). Here again, these 'passengers' would be mostly Portuguese, and occasionally some Spaniards and Italians. Missionaries were the last category of traveller — mostly Jesuits going to India, Malacca, Macao and Japan, and mostly Portuguese but including some Spaniards and Italians.

Not surprisingly, therefore, living conditions were indescribably bad, and the situation on board worsened when infection broke out in the crowded and fetid quarters. Toilet facilities were non-existent and the observance of elementary hygiene was minimal. As one experienced traveller noted, 'These ships are mighty foul and stink withal'. The supply of fresh meat and vegetables would soon run out, and the salted food would quickly putrefy in the scorching heat. Even the water supply was affected, for 'all the water in the ship stinketh, whereby men are forced to stop their noses when they drink'. The lack of fresh food brought on scurvy and dysentery, and disease spread rapidly in the rat-ridden quarters. Medical treatment was practically confined to blood-letting, and this tended to drain the patient of what little strength remained to him.

Possibly the most terrible case of disease occurred in 1567 when the new Viceroy of India sailed to take up his post. Of the 1,100 men on board, some 900, including the new Viceroy himself and the captain, had succumbed before the ship put in at Mozambique.

Provided all went well, the carrack would reach the Indian port of Goa in about five or six months, although many of the overloaded ships did not manage to complete even this first stage of the voyage. In the period 1550-1650 more than 112 ships were lost between Lisbon and Goa. But the passengers who reached India safely if not soundly were able to recover their health in the fine Royal Hospital in Goa. This was an institution which was especially equipped to care for sick travellers, and the arrival of the annual *nao* invariably meant an influx of diseased and sickly merchants and sailors. Those proceeding further east were given plenty of time to convalesce as they had to wait in any case for six or seven months for a suitable wind before resuming their travels.

In April or May of the following year the would-be visitor to Japan started out once more on the second stage of the long voyage. This part of the journey lasted about ten to twelve weeks and was not considered so dangerous as the Lisbon-Goa run. But as much of the route lay on or near the Equator, this lack of danger was cancelled out by the intolerable heat and the sheer monotony as the lumbering vessel slowly tacked backwards and forwards through the almost windless Malacca Straits. There was always, of course, the possibility of an attack by local pirates. In 1577, for example, a Portuguese carrack fought a seven-hour gun battle in the Straits of Singapore before it could continue on its way.

But even if there was no attack from outsiders, there was always the possibility of trouble on board. When tough soldiers, penniless adventurers and hardened traders were cooped up in intolerable conditions for months on end tempers were liable to fray and discipline among the motley crew break down. On such occasions, rioting and looting suddenly erupted on deck, and blood was shed and lives lost before order could be restored.

When the ship finally reached the Portuguese enclave of Macao on the coast of southern China, the traveller to Japan would have to summon up his patience once more and prepare for another long wait until the *nao* sailed in the following year. He was sometimes able to book passage on a Chinese junk and continue his voyage fairly rapidly. But this was chancing his luck because the small junks had a disconcerting habit of disappearing at sea, sunk without trace by the elements or by pirates. In 1599 a junk left Nagasaki for Macao carrying a large Asian crew, seventy Portuguese passengers and a huge fortune in silver crowns. The ship never reached its destination and no trace of it was ever discovered. Small wonder, then, that having journeyed safely thus far, the cautious traveller would prefer waiting for practically a year in Macao rather than risk sailing in a junk.

In July of the following year the last leg of the journey to Japan was begun. This was the shortest stage and lasted only three or four weeks, but at the same time it was also liable to be the most dangerous part of the voyage. The late summer and early autumn were the only times when a suitable wind would blow the carracks northwards to Japan. But this was also the storm season when torrential rains and mountainous seas, followed by the dreaded typhoons, caused havoc among the sailing ships.

In 1573 a richly-laden Portuguese ship was in sight of Japan when suddenly, on the morning of 21 July, a storm hit the vessel, overturned it in a matter of minutes, and only one survivor lived to tell the tale of the disaster. But sometimes the wooden ships managed to ride out the storms. A carrack was caught by a typhoon in 1578 as it was nearing Nagasaki. Its mast was snapped and the rudder lost; enormous waves crashed down on the ship, men were swept overboard, and, as one survivor later reported, 'Our blood froze and men became like statues'. The vessel was battered by the storm for three days, but, remarkable to say, the listing ship managed to remain afloat and eventually make its way to the Japanese coast.

A good number of Europeans, in fact, reached Japan as a result of storms. The first Europeans ever to set foot on Japanese soil were three Portuguese traders who were blown on to the small island of Tanegashima in 1543. Again in 1596 the Spanish galleon *San Felipe* was pounded for days by a storm and was forced to put in for an unscheduled and fateful stop-over in Japan. Only four years later the disabled Dutch ship, *Liefde,* carrying Will Adams, the first Englishman to reach Japan, drifted on to the Japanese coast after 'a wonderfull storm of winde, as ever I was in, with much raine'. Of the original 110 crew members, only eighteen survived; only six of the exhausted and emaciated crew were able to stand on their feet when the Japanese boarded the vessel.

Yet another Spanish ship met with disaster nine years later when the *San Francisco* en route to Mexico was caught in a typhoon, and the *hidalgo* Rodrigo de Vivero y Velasco, the former Governor of the Philippines, was unceremoniously dumped on the shore near present-day Tokyo and thus happily escaped the fate of most of the crew.

There were, of course, relatively prosperous voyages in which ships were not stricken with disease, attacked by pirates, grounded by shoals or battered by typhoons. But even if a passenger was fortunate enough to escape all these perils, his two-year voyage to Japan would still be full of hardship, anxiety and boredom. Small wonder, then, that European passengers for Japan included merchants and missionaries, but no tourists who had merely come for a ride and to enjoy a rest cure.

It is well to remember this when looking at the Southern Barbarian screens preserved in London, Lisbon and Paris. These colourful and decorative works vividly depict the hustle and bustle on board as the stately and beflagged carrack lies majestically at anchor in Nagasaki. But they tell only part of the story — the happy and successful part.

The Dutch through Japanese eyes

by Frits Vos

After 1639, when Japan sealed itself off from the outside world, the only foreign traders granted continued access to the country were the Dutch and the Chinese. From 1641, the Dutch were restricted to a settlement, or factory, on the islet of Deshima at the head of Nagasaki harbour, and the Chinese to a trading station in the city itself. Fan-shaped Deshima, connected to the mainland by a bridge, had been created in 1636 by the construction of a canal across a narrow peninsula. On the island, an area of little over three acres, were the dwellings, warehouses, and offices of the employees of the Dutch East India Company. There were usually ten to fifteen — never more than twenty — company officials in residence under a chief merchant or factor referred to by the Dutch as the *opperhoofd* (literally, main chief) and by the Japanese as the *kapitan* (from the Portuguese *capitão*).

Life on Deshima was far from pleasant, especially in the early years. The Dutch were constantly surrounded by spies. Since Christianity was severely proscribed in Japan, masters of incoming ships had to place all Bibles and other religious material under seal. Weapons and ammunition, and even the rudder and sails, were impounded until the vessel departed. The chief merchant alone was permitted to wear a sword, and then only on ceremonial occasions. In 1639, two years before the Dutch were confined to the island, the Japanese women to whom some of them were married had been sent, with their children, to Batavia (the present-day Jakarta), and thenceforward the company's officials were allowed to consort only with local prostitutes. Permission was rarely granted the Dutch to leave the island, which was guarded day and night. Once a year, and later in every four or five years, the tedium of their existence was relieved by a court journey to Edo, as Tokyo was then called. There, a chosen few paid homage to the *Shogun*, the administrative and military ruler of feudal Japan (the emperor, a sacrosanct figurehead, had his seat in Kyoto), presenting him with gifts which had often been ordered beforehand and were in fact a kind of tax levied for the privilege of being allowed to trade in the empire.

Up to 1854, when Japan reopened its doors to the West, the Dutch were tolerated in Nagasaki because they imported useful manufactured goods from Europe and the Indies and such colonial products as spices, tin, and mercury. Moreover, through the Dutch, the Japanese rulers kept themselves informed of events in the rest of the world.

The isolationist policy, which had been the aim of the Japanese government for some decades before it was fully implemented in 1639, marked the end of a period of fairly intensive contact with western culture. The Portuguese had held trading rights from 1543 to 1639, the Spaniards from 1592 to 1624, and the English from 1613 to 1623. Notwithstanding all the restrictions imposed during the period of seclusion, the Japanese, even some of the authorities, became increasingly interested in hearing about western scholarship and technology. As time went by and certain regulations were relaxed that interest developed further, culminating in the second half of the eighteenth century in a flowering of the study of the western sciences, which were referred to collectively as *Rangaku* — Hollandólogy or Dutch learning.

The word *Rangaku* covered a wide range of disciplines including medicine, astronomy, mathematics, botany, physics, geography, geodesy, and military science, especially ballistics. Less attention was devoted to European history and art. The scholars who specialised in these fields, all of which were studied in Dutch, were called *Rangakusha*, or Hollandologists. Japan's emergence as a major power in the second half of the nineteenth century is in large measure attributable to its rapid absorption and adaptation of western knowledge; the foundations of this intercultural borrowing process were laid by the *Rangakusha*.

However, we are concerned here not so much with the *Rangakusha* as with the opinions held by the Japanese regarding the Dutch — their appearance, their habits, their customs. But first, some further information about life on Deshima, particularly about the few opportunities for relaxation enjoyed by the Dutch community there.

The court journey to Edo, for instance — a round-trip of approximately thirteen hundred miles overland — required weeks of preparation and even longer on the way. It took place at the beginning of the Japanese lunar year or some time between 20 January and 19 February by our calendar. For the occasion, the chief merchant was accorded the status of a *daimyo*, or feudal lord, and travelled with a handful of his compatriots and a large Japanese retinue. Though all this imposed a heavy strain on the factory's resources, and travellers were subjected to constant control and supervision, the length of the journey and the unusual chances it afforded for sightseeing and diversion meant that in many ways it was truly pleasurable.

For their love life the Dutch on Deshima were dependent on Marúyama, the licensed brothel quarter of Nagasaki, which provided the lonely Hollanders with sweet companions to while away their idle hours.

Of the holidays observed by the Dutch, New Year is of particular interest. Various Japanese officials and the Japanese interpreters were invited to a banquet that began at midday. A Japanese document dating from 1818 lists the many dishes served on such an occasion by the factory's Indonesian servants: soup, eggs, mushrooms, chicken, duck, halibut, sea bream, salmon, beef, pork, a boar's head, ham, turnips, Dutch vegetables, and a variety of pastries. The main beverages were *zenefuru* (geneva, Dutch gin), *biiru* (beer), and *araki* (arrack). The word *biiru* is still used in modern Japanese, as is also *kohii*, the rendering of the Dutch word for coffee.

Another annual celebration is especially interesting. It was known as *Oranda-toshi* (Dutch winter solstice). Having expelled the Portuguese and Spanish for overzealous proselytising, the Japanese permitted the Dutch to remain in their country only on condition that no attempt was made to practise the Christian religion or to attract converts. For the sake of trade, the East India Company ordered this rule to be scrupulously observed. Inspired, however, by the fact that the Chinese in Nagasaki celebrated the winter solstice towards the end of December, the Dutch on Deshima conceived the idea of using this holiday as a cover for their own Christmas celebration, modest though that might be. The local inhabitants took part in the festivities, assembling at dawn on the appointed day for what was called the procession of Dutch ships. Some time earlier, the tradesmen who supplied the Dutch with their daily needs had grouped together with the artisans who did all sorts of odd jobs on Deshima to make wooden models of Dutch ships, which were now carried in procession to the sound of gongs. The revellers made their way to Deshima to offer their best wishes to the chief merchant and his staff. The model ships were presented to the Dutch, who in turn bestowed small gifts of money upon their visitors. And again a banquet was held in honour of the local officials and interpreters. Remarkably enough, the Japanese, otherwise so watchful for signs of the forbidden Christian practices, never seem to have suspected the true reason for these particular festivities.

The Japanese view of the Dutch and the Netherlands can best be prefaced by a few excerpts from one of the earliest treatises on the subject, *Todo shinden* (A True Account of the Supreme Way), by Ando Shoeki (?1701-58). In his work, Ando uses his own interpretation of the Chinese philosophy concerning the action of the five elements (fire, water, wood, metal, and earth) to explain various phenomena. The geographical location of the Occident means that the Netherlands is completely dominated by the physical principle of the element metal — that element which corresponds to the West, autumn, cold, sensuality, righteousness, and so on. He writes:

'The people average six feet in height. Because of the prevalence of the physical principle of the element metal, the essence of autumn, the same principle is strongly at work in their bodies. Its unyielding nature obliges them to keep up their strength with meat, which they eat at every meal. They brew strong drink, which they keep for a time before consuming it. The influence of the physical principle causes wheat, which is in affinity with it, to grow excellently in the Netherlands, and consequently the Dutch always eat bread made from wheat.

'The pupils of their eyes are clear and light red, like those of monkeys. Their eyes are set deep in their round faces; their teeth are exceedingly white. They are very partial to tobacco and always carry the instruments needed for smoking in a pouch on the hip ... They are blessed by nature with wondrous skills of many kinds and have an inborn self-restraint and sense of justice.'

The book from which the above passage is drawn and other Japanese works contain enough material for a list of misconceptions about the Dutch. They are not blessed with longevity. Though Ando explained this on 'scientific' grounds, another writer, Hirata Atsutane (1776-1843), often called the theologian of *Shinto* (Japan's Ethnocentric religion) ascribed it to their addiction to sexual excesses and drink. 'It is just as rare for a Dutchman to reach fifty,' he writes, 'as for a Japanese to reach a hundred.' Their height is always wildly exaggerated, the prevailing opinion being that they are taller than other (or normal) people. They have eyes like animals, and no heels. Hirata states that their eyes resembled those of a dog, and goes on to say that 'because the back part of their feet does not appear to touch the ground, they attach wooden heels to their shoes.' 'To urinate,' according to Hirata and others, 'they lift up one leg after the manner of a dog.' The stereotype so often held by one people of another's sexual potency was in evidence here as well, it being widely believed in Japan that the Dutch possessed remarkable sexual powers which they heightened still further with potions and the like.

In his *Ransetsu benwaku* (Corrections of Erroneous Theories Concerning the Dutch; 1788), Otsuki Gentaku (1757-1827) rebutted such popular fallacies, though without much success, as is apparent from the writings of Hirata and others.

Ando Shoeki had a very high opinion of the sexual morality of the Dutch. In his treatise on the Supreme Way he dwells on the subject at some length:

'Their way of marriage is truly correct. Once a man is married he does not mix with other women, nor does his wife meet other men. They observe the mutual love of husband and wife and have no affection for others. When a man without a wife becomes involved with someone else's wife, his kinsfolk get together and kill him; and when a widow becomes involved with someone else's husband, her family gets together and kills her ... It may happen that during his stay in Nagasaki, a man who has a wife (in the Netherlands) will forget himself and have dealings with Japanese harlots. When he returns to his country ... his wife will immediately know this by the expression on his face and will hurry to inform his kinsfolk, who will get together and kill him at once. The ability to know such a thing immediately is a characteristic of the people of that country, which in this respect is superior to all other countries.'

The *Rangaku* period coincided with a change in the Japanese philosophy of life, with not only the *Rangakusha* but many other scholars as well turning steadily further away from the culture of China which had hitherto been held in such veneration. But with one or two exceptions, their admiration for the West remained limited to its scientific and technological achievements. The principle consciously followed in the intercultural borrowing process set in motion by the Meiji Restoration of 1868 found clear expression in the slogan *wakon yosai*: Japanese spirit and western learning.

The promise of greater things to come
by Frank Ashton-Gwatkin

I first saw Japan during the latter half of April 1913, at the age of twenty-four, from the deck of a P. & O. steamer travelling from Shanghai to Kobe. In that dawn of a new life I saw the strait between Shimonoseki and Moji heavy with history — past and future: Shimonoseki bombarded by foreign warships in 1863, and, in 1894, scene of the signing of the Sino-Japanese Treaty, which recognized Japan's military power; and the high chimneys of the iron- and steelworks of Moji, big with Japan's future as a worldwide industrial and commercial empire.

After a brief stop-over at Shimonoseki the steamer took us to Kobe through the Inland Sea — one of the world's wonders of delicate beauty — an accurate reflection of a hundred thousand Japanese drawings and prints — with pine clad islands, temples and *torii*.

The landing at Kobe made no remembered impression; then embarkation on board the express train for Tokyo.

There I met Japan in person. He was seated in the observation car — a figure in Japanese dress — fanning himself in an armchair. A middle-aged man, rotund, dignified and friendly. He spoke fluent and humorous English. Yes, he had spent

Plate 6: *Young men parade the local shrine, Omykoshi, round the streets for the summer festival.*

Plate 7: *Infants divided up into colour groups to match with their teachers, enjoying an afternoon out in Nara.*

severel years in England when he was quite young, near the Crystal Palace. Yes, he had many friends in the British Embassy.

At Shidzuoka station a large and officious-looking deputation was lined up on the platform. My new friend moved to the door and stepped down from the carriage. The deputation bowed; my friend bowed. The leading deputy made a speech; my friend replied. Renewed bowing. The train was held up for ten minutes. As he departed, my friend handed me his card and said, by way of explanation: 'Prince Tokugawa Iyesato — President of the House of Peers.' He remained my friend for the next twenty years.

It was an auspicious arrival in Japan.

At Yokohama station three Englishmen got into the train; they were Edward Crowe, Colin Davidson and George Sansom — the three stars of the Japan Consular Service at that time, of which I was now a member. They were on their way to some Embassy function that evening. Crowe was the Commercial Attaché. Later he was to be Permanent Secretary of the Department of Overseas Trade in London, then on retirement a tycoon in the City. He was to die suddenly and delightfully as he rose from a bridge-table in Cairo. Colin Davidson was then Vice-Consul in Yokohama. More than any of us he had achieved a degree of friendly intimacy with the Japanese, who included ex-*daimyos* and their wives and children. He was by nature a courtier; and most suitably was attached to the Prince of Wales' suite during his state visit to Japan.

George Sansom was a scholar — one of the greatest of orientalists and Japanologues. He was to write the grammar of the written language and the authoritative history of Japan in three volumes. He ought to have been Ambassador to Tokyo. As it was, he became Professor in Columbia and in Stamford Universities and he died in the USA.

All three were my life-long friends.

Our arrival at Tokyo was a disappointment. There was no red carpet laid down for the three 'student interpreters', as we were called. There was not even room ready in the Embassy; nor were we considered valuable enough for rooms at the Imperial Hotel — the only first-class hotel then existing in the Japanese capital, built by Frank Lloyd, but rebuilt in 1967. Instead, we were assigned to the Hibiya Hotel, a Japanese venture built and furnished in what the owners imagined to be 'foreign' style, directed to attract the would-be European section of the modern-minded Japanese, the *haikara* world — a word which no doubt has vanished now but which then, being derived from the 'high collar' fancied at the time by gilded youth, had come to be an adjective connoting all that was smart, chic, up to date and progressive.

Next day, we were received at the British Embassy. The Embassy compound in Kojimachi-ku was like a slice of Wimbledon flown out to Tokyo on a magic, green carpet. All the buildings were of red brick. The Ambassador's house looked suitable for a late Victorian tycoon. Scattered about the domain were separate houses for the Counsellor, the Japanese (i.e. the Japanese-speaking) Counsellor, the First Secretary, the Second Secretary, and the student interpreters — five of us living together in a mess. There had once been a tower. It overlooked the grounds of the Imperial Palace and had given offence to the Japanese people and also to the gods of Japan who cast it down in an earthquake. It was never rebuilt, but a mound with a flagstaff on it marked the place where it once stood.

Such was the centre of my existence during my first two years in Japan. It was not noticeably Japanese, except for the Japanese clerks, interpreters, teachers, tradespeople and domestics who frequented the compound.

The Tokyo of 1913 was neither a beautiful nor a dignified city. It was more of a conglomeration of squat, wooden Japanese towns clustered around the spacious

Plate 8: Students in Nagasaki performing the Dragon Dance during the Okunchi festival in October.

43

enclosure, where, ringed by a deep moat, banked by sloping walls of cyclopean stones, and draped with a cape of evergreen forestry, crouched unseen the palace of the mysterious Emperor. The palace, or *gosho* (honourable place), was the most impressive feature of the city, though, or perhaps because, it blocked all swift access between the four quarters of the compass. And I imagine that this is still the case.

The new central railway station was opened before I left Japan. But, in 1913, we still used the old station in Shimbashi beyond the *geisha* quarter, and from there the central thoroughfare, the Ginza, led more or less straight through the city to the notorious quarters of Asakusa and the Yoshiwara.

There were a few modern shops on the Ginza such as the excellent Maruzen bookshop and the admirable Mitsukoshi store. But the network of shops and businesses and family dwellings in the numerous side streets and along the canals might have come straight out of the pages of Hokusai's engravings Beautiful, no; but very picturesque. Horse-drawn vehicles — a certain number of farm carts and sanitary waggons with wooden buckets full of sewage — very few cars — a motorcar was an event; thousands of rickshaws and thousands of bicycles.

And the trams! Grumbling and hissing and clattering along all the main streets with clots of humanity clinging to them like swarms of bees until the inevitable *shadan* (electricity failure) brought the whole system to a stand-still.

My duty, for which I received lodging and a small amount of pocket money, was to learn the Japanese language and to study the ways in which the Japanese lived and thought.

I was engaged in this study for over six years; two in the Tokyo Embassy, three in the Consulate General in Yokohama, and one and a half in Singapore. It was hard work, for the language (both spoken and written) is extremely difficult. There was no school, and the official teachers — Kubota, Saito and Sekine — had to be taught (by us)

Kinoshita Takeji (left) with his cousin in Ashton-Gwatkin's room

how to teach. We were precluded by poverty and by the unwritten rules of the Embassy from adopting the best way of language study — namely by procuring a Japanese mistress. There has been no Madame Butterfly in my life, alas!

So poverty and chastity went hand in hand.

Our other Embassy duty was to act as clerks, typists, and cypherers in the diplomatic chancery. This, too, was a useful education. One learned a little of what diplomacy is — i.e. the first line of our country's defence — and of how it works, its conventions and technicalities.

As for diplomatic life as popular imagination portrays it — the balls, the dinner parties, the cocktail parties, I saw very little of this. I did not even learn to play bridge!

I was in Japan during the pause which followed the exhausting triumph of the war against Russia. A triumph which recognized Japan as a major military and naval power. She was allied with Great Britain 'to maintain peace in Asia'. The United States, though potentially a great power, had not yet exerted herself as such.

Japan, therefore, had joined, as a junior member, a club consisting of Great Britain, France, Germany, Russia, Austria and Italy; and her reflexes, at that time, were European rather than American. Her big cities, Tokyo, Yokohama, Osaka, Kobe, were beginning to have a somewhat European aspect, large buildings but no skyscrapers; whisky and *ramune* (lemonade), but no cocktails or Coca-Cola.

Great Britain was, in Japanese eyes, the most important foreign country; and was she not her ally? In her emulation of *Great* Britain, Japan had started to call herself *Great* Japan (*Dai* Nihon). Great Britain's possible rival, Germany — there were many admirers of Germany in Japan, especially among the military — was to be defeated in the war of 1914-18. Thereafter the 'liberal' wing, if it can be called such, gained prestige in the political world under the Kenseito party and such leaders as Hara, Kato Takkaki, Inukai and Takahashi Dan.

The seizure of the German fortress of Tsingtao in 1914 was followed — to Japanese minds quite logically — by an advance of Japanese influence over North China, as declared in the 21 Demands of 1915, which, if accepted in full, would have reduced North China including Peking to the status of a semi-protectorate of Japan.

The blatancy of the Demands alerted popular opinion in the US and Canada, and to a lesser extent in Great Britain. The Japanese withdrew their more extreme demands. This episode was the most important political event in Far Eastern History during my period in Japan; and indeed it was one of the turning points in Japanese — and Chinese — history.

In Tokyo, in the foreign community, we were well aware of what was happening; and out of that realization two schools of thought developed. One school looked to the Anglo-Japanese Alliance as a check to Japan's military ambitions in China; the other school saw Japanese policy as utilizing the Alliance as a screen behind which to pursue those ambitions. The Alliance, therefore, so they thought, should be dropped or modified.

This was the situation which I found in London when I came to work as a Japan specialist in the Foreign Office towards the end of 1919.

As time went on, of course, I had the opportunity to discover other parts of Japan, including Kyoto and Nara — one of the loveliest corners of the globe, which, thank God and the gods (Shinto) have survived the war. I visited Osaka and Nagoya when writing a report on the Japanese toy industry for Edward Crowe, the Commercial Attaché. I also visited Nikko, a romantic spot, famous for the tombs and temples of the Tokugawa *shoguns* and there I met again Prince Tokugawa, arrayed as a Shinto priest, 'in my fancy dress', he explained to me; he was in attendance on some family ceremony.

From Nikko, I remember, I went on for some twelve miles or so, up into the mountains past the famous Kegon waterfall to the Lake of Chuzenji, where the summer resort of the British and several other foreign embassies was located. I stayed as a guest in the *besso* (country house) of two of our secretaries and tried to learn how to steer a small sailing-boat called a 'lark' across the lake. From Chuzenji I visited one of Japan's last gold mines.

But my first two years were mainly devoted to my Japanese studies. This was my job; it was also my hobby. I was fascinated by this world so new and all. And the imprint of Japan has been left upon me for the rest of my life.

This imprint was first due to those two years in Tokyo; to daily absorption in a Japanese atmosphere; to the company of colleagues who had specialized in Japanese life — especially Parlett, Hobart-Hampden, Sansom, Davidson and Crowe. Not least, and with a resounding note of gratitude, to Kinoshita Takeji — furniture merchant of Tora-no-Mon in Tokyo. This true friend made it his passion to teach me Japanese. He drew up a phrase book for me in three different strata:

Polite: *Oide kudasaimashi*: Please come (to superiors)
Ordinary: *Irrasshai* or *Oide nasai*: Come along (to equals)
Common: *Kochi ye koi*: Come here (to servants and intimate friends)

He took me with him on a three weeks tour, which included a visit to his cousins — farmers and small landowners in Shinano Province, and a long weekend of *kenbutsu* (looking at things) by the unspoiled seaside at Atami beyond Hakone. With another cousin, a Tokyo businessman, we also went behind the scenes of a *Kabuki* theatre to watch a very famous actor (Utaemon I think) making up for a female rôle.

I was present at two historical State funerals: that of the Empress Dowager, Emperor Meiji's Consort; and that of Tokugawa Keiki, last of the Shoguns to have actually occupied the Regent's throne. He had resigned, not unwillingly, in 1868, and had lived in quiet retirement until 1914. My friend, Colin Davidson, had been to visit him from time to time, and had received from him a souvenir autograph. It read:

From the midst of tranquillity
I observe the world.

I climbed to the top of Fujiyama in company with my two fellow students, Fowke and de Bunsen, and with that saintly poet, Cecil Boutflower, Bishop in South Tokyo.

It was an exhausting clamber rather than a climb, and it was rewarded by the sight of the whole country being unpacked at dawn from layers of cotton-wool clouds. The descent was even more painful, for the sharp ashes had ripped the soles off my shoes.

Among the people I met in those early years was Lord Bryce discoursing about the *ginko* tree, and Sir William Watts, naval architect of the 'Dreadnought', together with his Belgian wife and their daughter, Louise Trevelyan, who was married to Freeman Trevelyan, agent in Japan for the Armstrong-Whitworth armament firm.

An early notable event was that of the naval scandals, following which Trevelyan of Armstrongs and his competitor, Winder of Vickers, left Japan in a great hurry. A report had appeared in the Press of the enormous bribes paid to Japanese politicians and admirals in connection with the contracts for the battleship *Kongo*. There were three or four suicides; and the government of Admiral Yamamoto Gombei fell from office. And so a new word was added to Japanese slang — *gombeijiru*, to bribe and corrupt on a large scale. There was never another prevailingly *Satsuma* government in Japan; and the reins of ultimate power fell increasingly into the hands of the Army politicians and the ambitious traditions of the Choshu clan — with dire results in the long run.

The 'elder statesmen' — the *Genro* — still had the last word in those days. There were three of them left — Yamagata (the aged war-god of the Russo-Japanese War),

Matsukata and Saionji, who was younger than the other two. I once had the distinction of conducting the old Field-Marshal to his box of honour for some celebration in the Imperial Theatre; and Prince Saionji I met twice — once in Singapore on his way to the Paris Peace Conference (he was accompanied by the beautiful O Hana-san and by his Private Secretary, Mr Yoshida Shigeru, later to become the great post-war Prime Minister) and again in Paris itself, where he told me that he had been there as a student at the time of the Commune (1871) and had stood on a barricade shouting for *Liberté*.

The next great event was the outbreak of war in Europe. I was sent away in a steam-yacht de luxe, the *Mekong*, lent by a French Duke to the British Government. Our instructions were to act as a wireless station in the harbour of Shanghai. I was to be cypher-clerk and interpreter, if required. That adventure only lasted for three weeks. Meanwhile the Japanese had come into the war and had taken over all operations in the Far East.

I returned in the Tokyo chancery, and I shared in decyphering the long telegram in which the British Government offered to take over several divisions of the Japanese Army (specifying rates of pay, pensions, etc, in great detail) for service on the Western Front. Before we had finished the telegram we could see that it was a non-starter. And sure enough, when our Ambassador presented it to the Minister of Foreign Affairs, he was told rather curtly that the Japanese Army was there for the defence of the nation; her soldiers were not mercenaries.

But within the limits of the Alliance Treaty Japan carried out her obligations. She declared war on Germany; sent an army to China to reduce the German fortress of Tsingtao; sent her ships to the South Seas to take over the German islands (Carolines and Marshalls) and to guard the British port of Singapore and all the sea-routes east of the Indian Ocean.

After the Battle of the Falkland Islands and the sinking of the 'Emden', the Pacific Ocean and the South Seas and the whole of Asia except Mesopotamia and Palestine were saved from the struggle of World War I, until, in 1917, the Bolshevik Revolution opened a new and unexpected chapter in world history.

Meanwhile my private world was also changing. I had moved from the Embassy at Tokyo to the Consulate-General in Yokohama. My setting and my friends had changed; and I had married my Australian fiancée early in April, 1915. Embassy typings and cypherings had changed into the day-to-day activity of a consular post in wartime — passports (a new institution), certificates of origin (to check absence of enemy interest in commercial transactions) and so on.

Since those days Yokohama has been twice destroyed — first, by earthquake in 1923 and, secondly, by war. Motomachi, Bentendori, Honmoku-cho (or Chinatown), the Bund, the hatoba, the creek, the bridge by the French Consulate-General, the steep hill up to the Bluff where one had to get two rickshawmen, one to pull and one to push, up to the top where stood St George's Church and where Nancy and I were married.

For three years I saw little of the Japanese, or indeed of the foreign community — except in my office. Our life was constricted by poverty and wartime conditions. But we did save up enough for three weeks' holiday in Peking. And we used to go for drives (horse-drawn) along the coast of Tomioka, and for frequent excursions (by train) to Tokyo.

I took a volunteer job in Tokyo as assistant on the staff of *The New East*, a bi-monthly, bi-lingual magazine financed by the British Government to stimulate interest in things British among the Japanese intelligentsia (and vice versa). The Editor was John Robertson-Scott, a well-known journalist of the W. T. Stead, pre-

Harmsworth period, who was in Japan at the outbreak of war, accumulating material for a book on Japanese agriculture. Over six foot tall, with the mane and beard of a prophet, inspired by the fervent faith of a convinced rationalist, John — with his wife Elspet and his sister-in-law Elizabeth, who were artistic and fey — created *The New East*, as later in England they were to create *The Countryman*. They were all professional journalists; and in their book-and-paper-littered house in Azabu-ku, Tokyo, they taught me a smattering of newspaper technicalities, while I helped as office-boy and translator. Yes, and I contributed notes and articles, which were paid for, to the review, and for the first time since my Newdigate poem I saw myself in print with ideas of authorship beginning to shape my dreams. At the *New East* office, too, I met young intellectual Japan (Yanagi and Yanagita, also Lafcadio Hearn's widow and son), also visitors from abroad, such as Langdon Warner from the Boston Museum of Art, and James Murdoch, the old hermit historian, and Bernard Leach, the young artist-potter. It was through an introduction from Robertson-Scott that in Peking I came to know the famous Dr George Morrison.

There was another nobly-bearded figure, another prophet, I was privileged to meet — not rationalist this one, but universally idealist — Rabindranath Tagore. As a famous Asiatic personality he was on a State visit to Japan, and was lodged in the villa of Mr Hara, a silk tycoon, at Ichi-no-Tani near Yokohama. He began every day, he said, with two hours' meditation — hanging his physical body up 'like a cloak on a clothes-peg'. I have never been able to achieve that, but I am very grateful to my guardian spirits that I have known Tagore.

Soon after this peaceful visit, the Great Revolution broke out over distracted Europe; and I was sent by the Embassy to find another visitor, this time at the Grand Hotel, Yokohama — Admiral Kolchak. I was to hand him an envelope containing his commission to restore law and order in Russia. A noble and tragic figure charged with a hopeless task and a terrible end.

Yokohama, meanwhile, was flooded with a double tide of Russians — one flowing east to west (revolutionaries from exile summoned to their sudden Paradise, among them Léon Trotsky from Canada), and one from west to east (refugees fleeing from Hell). I saw more of the latter — in my office — asking for visas; but I heard plenty of the former in the apartment house where I was living — talking, talking incessantly all through the night.

Out of this apartment house — Bankokukwan, the International Building — where we had lived for a year or more, we were blown not by a Revolution but by a typhoon, a Great Wind indeed which wrecked every window in the flat, and sent us rain-lashed and shivering in the early morning to take refuge in the Oriental Hotel.

America had now come into the war, so we knew we must win; Russia had collapsed, so we knew we might lose.

Japan, not unnaturally, had profited by the war. Prices had risen and much money had been made — by the old-established firms and by the new rich, the profiteers or *narikin* (become-money) as they were called in Japan. Japanese enterprise was extending overseas — nowhere more than in Malaysia and Indonesia (then the Dutch East Indies) or as the Japanese called it *Nanyo*, the Southern Ocean. The British authorities in Singapore were puzzled and alarmed by this invasion. The Japanese were buying up rubber estates, offices and private houses. They had their own club and newspaper; and every Japanese carried his camera. The GOC Singapore, Major-General Sir Dudley Ridout, appealed to the Embassy, Tokyo, asking if he could have the services of an interpreter, Japanese-speaking, to advise him on Japanese questions, and especially on the great question 'What are the Japanese up to?'.

I was offered the job, and I accepted it at once. Who would not have done so? I envisaged a permanent future in Singapore as a kind of 'Japanese Secretary' to the Straits Government. But no, said Hobart-Hampden, the Japanese Secretary in Tokyo: 'It will be an episode in one act'.

And so it was, but not without consequences. I had been in Japan for just about five years; and in April, 1918 we left Yokohama for Hong Kong, where we changed boats for the last lap to Singapore.

I had finished my apprenticeship. I now had a job of my own and to me (at least) a clear direction. I had learned sufficient Japanese to carry on a conversation and to read a newspaper or a novel; and the Japanese no longer appeared to me to be 'inscrutable'. I was beginning to understand the real meaning of history, diplomacy, power and policy. This lesson was impressed upon me when I saw the three great, grey Japanese men-of-war guarding Singapore harbour. Moreover, I was now married, and I had a companion and lover with whom to share my life. I had half the typescript of my first novel in my box, and unbounded self-confidence. I was thirty years old.

2 Way of life

Life-line *by Arnold Toynbee*

Is Japan's way of life changing now in all fields, or only in some fields? And, if in all fields, are there significant differences in the pace and the degree of change as between one field and another? In order to try to answer these questions, we must survey the several fields separately and must then try to take a comprehensive view. The fields that it may be useful to distinguish in considering Japan's prospects are the cultural, social, industrial and political.

In the cultural field, we may begin with drama and music. I have seen performances of *Kabuki* and *Nō* plays, and I have been interested in the attitude of the audience, as well as in the art of the plays and the artistry of the actors. My impression is that a present-day Japanese audience's appreciation of *Kabuki* — and of *Nō*, a fortiori — is not unlike a present-day western audience's appreciation of a classical Greek play performed either in the original Greek or in a translation into one or other of the modern western languages. In both cases, the audience is limited to a highly sophisticated minority of the population, and the pleasure that they derive from seeing the play performed is, we might almost say, 'archaeological'. They obtain intellectual satisfaction from their mastery of a technique that, by now, is long ago obsolete. I think the Elizabethan drama is more alive than this for present-day English-speaking people, and the seventeenth-century drama for present-day French-speaking people. When witnessing the performance of one of Shakespeare's or Moliere's plays, they are not conscious, to the same degree, that what they are seeing is an artificial revival of something antique.

As regards music, I am no judge; but, the first time that I heard national Japanese instrumental music and singing (it was in 1929), I was reminded of Turkish music and singing. I felt, whether correctly or mistakenly, that the Japanese and Turkish modes were akin to each other, and that they differed from the modern western mode in an identical way. I find it all the more remarkable that today there is, in Japan, a public for classical western music. Western musicians who have performed in Japan in recent years have told me that they have found audiences there not only enthusiastic but also manifestly appreciative of the fine points of this exotic art.

Are the Japanese likely to retain their links with the major expressions of their cultural past? And what happens to a society that loses touch with its own past? In the Soviet Union, where a deliberate attempt has been made to break with much of the pre-Communist Russian past, there has been no inhibition in the reading of nineteenth-century Russian literature. On the other hand, in Turkey, a sharp break with the past has been produced by the secularization of the state, in which Islam was formerly the established religion, and also by the substitution of the Latin for the Arabic alphabet. Japan, so far, has retained her two *kana* scripts (*hira-gana* and *kata-kana*); she has not even given up the practice of using a certain number of Chinese characters (ideograms) in the Chinese way. For a Japanese child, learning to read and write is more difficult than it is for a western child — or for a Turkish child before Turkey changed its alphabet; yet, in talking to Japanese children, I have had the impression that they find learning to write more enjoyable than western children find it. For a Japanese child, writing is more like drawing and painting. The script that they are mastering is not just utilitarian; it is also beautiful; and its beauty appeals aesthetically to the learner.

All the same, Japan's break with her past is great enough to raise the question of the consequences. What, then, is the price of radical cultural changes? I suggest that this is not an exclusively Japanese question. It is a question that concerns all the peoples of the world, including the westerner.

Let me go back to the case of western classical music. This is a very recent western art. It did not blossom till the seventeenth century, and the latest of the titanic western composers, Brahms, lived into the eighteen-nineties. Brahms' lifetime just overlapped with mine. Yet, when today a western audience listens to classical music, is not its relation to this music really much the same as a contemporary Japanese audience's relation to it? Is not western classical music equally alien to a present-day western ear? And is not the appreciation of this classical western art attained today, in Japan and in the West alike, by a deliberate act of self-attunement? The point that I am making is that the West's revolutionisation of human life has been so violent that it has turned the West's life, as well as the rest of mankind's life, upside down. I cannot foresee what is going to happen to a society that has lost touch with its own past. But I guess that this still unanswered question about the future is no longer specifically Japanese or Russian or Turkish; it is now a western question too.

If I am right about this, 'westernisation' is no longer an adequate word for describing a global revolutionary change which has engulfed the West itself. The word 'modernisation' is more apt. Moreover, though it was the West that initiated this world-wide transformation of mankind's way of life, the West is no longer the sole revolutionary agent. Other parts of the world — Russia, Africa, East Asia — are now making original and characteristic contributions of their own to the new common way of life which is replacing the virtually self-contained regional civilizations of the past. But how rapidly, and to what extent, are these traditional civilizations going to be superseded? Though global modernism is a powerful solvent, local tradition is a potent conservative force. Japanese society has been hierarchical since the dawn of Japanese history. This traditional structure of Japanese society survived the introduction of Buddhism and of Chinese manners, customs and institutions; it lived through the rise of Japanese feudalism and its subsequent isolation during the Tokugawa regime; it also survived the Meiji Restoration. Will it prove to have survived the catastrophe of 1945, which was followed by the first foreign military occupation in Japan's history?

It is not yet possible to answer this question more than tentatively. The Japanese style of social intercourse, marked by a distinct formality and courtesy, still surprises westerners. Even after the Japanese moved out of farms and castles into factories and offices, the hierarchical structure of their society appears to have endured and is clearly evident today. Traditional courtesy is enshrined in the language. When I have given lectures in Japan, I have found that it has taken the interpreter an hour and a half to say in Japanese what I myself had taken one hour to say in English. The idiom of western languages is concise, because it is blunt. To talk in this western style in Japanese would, I guess, sound excruciatingly discourteous to Japanese ears.

Superficially, then, the traditional Japanese way of life looks as if it is still strongly entrenched. Yet I have my doubts. The translation of a lecture is, after all, an academic exercise in which tradition is on advantageous ground for maintaining itself. But in what kind of language do Japanese technicians think and talk when they are making blueprints for computers or for mammoth tankers? I suspect that, for such purposes, they use a radically modernized Japanese, an anglicized Japanese, perhaps even English itself — a fact which could throw light on the future.

The business activities by which we earn our living are on the surface of life. It is our personal relations with each other which reach to the roots of life — especially such fundamental relations as those between husband and wife, between parents and children, between young men and women before marriage. I have the impression that, in this field — and it is a crucial field — Japanese life has been changing rather fast since 1945 — leaving behind hierarchical tradition. The mother has gained power in the family at the father's expense; the parents' relation to the children has become less authoritarian; marriageable boys and girls have a more free-and-easy relationship with each other now than in the past. This would mean that in Japan, as well as in countries with a less hierarchical tradition, conservatism is now in retreat, and is fighting merely a rearguard action.

The industrialization of Japan's economic life has been an astonishing tour de force. The Meiji Restoration eclipsed Peter the Great's technological revolution in eighteenth-century Russia. The explosion of Japan's productive power since the end of the Second World War has now dwarfed the Meiji Restoration. In just over a century, Japan has made herself into the second greatest industrial country in the world. She has outdistanced West Germany and the Soviet Union and has become the United States' most formidable competitor. Japan has achieved this economic triumph by plunging headlong into modern industrialism. She is now as deeply committed to this way of life as the West's most highly industrialized countries. But what are the prospects for this industrialized minority of mankind into which Japan has deliberately and successfully assimilated herself?

Japan has reached her dizzy industrial peak just at the moment when the industrialized countries have become aware that they have involved themselves in grave trouble. They have snatched the huge profits of technology at the price of incurring debts of a corresponding magnitude to Nature; and Nature is now presenting the bill. Pre-Industrial Revolution Man recognized and reverenced Nature as his divine mother — an attitude expressed in Shinto — and the pre-Christian and pre-Islamic religions of the western end of the Old World and of pre-Columbian America were counterparts of Shinto. Nature-worship was, indeed, the world-wide religion of agricultural, pastoral, hunting and food-gathering Man. The peoples plunging into industrialism have taken to treating Nature as a utility to be exploited, and Nature is now retaliating. The first items on her bill are pollution and the consumption of irreplaceable resources — demonstrating that she is a goddess after all.

The industrialized peoples do not know how they are going to clear their formidable debit account with Nature. It is conceivable that, at the height of their industrial powers, they may be prostrated by a paralytic stroke. If this nemesis does overtake them, there may be a dramatic reversal of fortunes between this stricken industrialized minority of mankind and the still uncompromised peasant majority. When Japan dived into the deep waters of industrialization, China stayed dithering on the brink, scorned and ill-treated by the industrialized western peoples, and finally by Japan too. By comparison with Japan, was China weak-willed? Or was she perhaps far-sighted? In either case, she has proved to be fortunate; for today the peoples who have plunged into industrialism up to the neck are discovering, with horror, that these waters are contaminated. Meanwhile, China has scarcely wetted her feet.

China has waited long enough to learn from the West's and Japan's experiences, that reckless industrialization is perilous, and, in the light of this lesson, China may now decide to treat Nature with greater forbearance and discrimination. She may perhaps adopt a modicum of Japanese and western technology, but she may graft this on to the traditional peasant economy instead of obliterating her fields under a super-structure of autobahns and factories that are too heavy a load for the earth to bear. One smaller East-Asian country, Burma, has already adopted this circumspect policy; if China, too, were to adopt it, she might eventually have the rest of the world at her feet.

A country cannot permanently reject its geopolitical destiny. Japan is East Asian, as inevitably as Britain is West European. In East Asia, which is half the world, China has always been the Middle Kingdom. And Japan's relations with China will be decisive for Japan's future; she cannot afford to let these relations remain unfriendly. However, the initiative in deciding whether China and Japan are to be friends or enemies may lie, not in Japan's hands, but in China's.

You and me *by Chie Nakane*

'How have you been recently?' (*sonogo ikaga-desuka*) and 'I'm sorry I haven't had a chance to see you sooner' (*gobusata itashimashita*) are favourite forms of greeting among Japanese when meeting friends and acquaintances. In fact, the frequency of meeting in Japanese society reflects the strength (or weakness) of a relationship. A good personal relationship is built up by frequent and direct contact. In conversation with an acquaintance about a mutual friend, for example, you would define your 'closeness' to that friend by recalling to your listener how often you meet the friend. In turn, your acquaintance could express his more distant, less involved attitude by answering 'I haven't seen him for such a long time; I've really no idea what he's doing these days.' The true significance of this 'meeting' concept in relationships might be explained as follows. Regular meetings, regular communication, automatically means a regular and reliable exchange of information. Thus those who meet regularly normally develop a close and trusting relationship. In fact, it is quite typical for the average Japanese to try and establish daily contact with his close friends; and his close friends invariably will be found among his fellow workers at his own place of work (since they present themselves as the obvious group of people with whom he has dealings all the time).

Within the Japanese sociological world there are three clearly distinguished categories concerning interrelationships. The first category involves those in one's own immediate group — one's closest friends. The second covers all those who share the same background and have things in common. The third category covers everybody else. In a rural setting, for example, the first category would include all the other villagers in the neighbourhood. Since a typical Japanese village ia made up of a distinct grouping of households (from just a handful to perhaps several hundred) the villagers as a group form a closely knit society and take part in a whole variety of communal activities. The second category would cover neighbouring villagers (in another area close by). Here, one's kith and kin might be included, schoolfriends and others in business, commerce or politics who share one's interests. The number of people in this circle can quickly be enlarged, of course, through introductions by the existing group to other people within the circle with whom one has not yet become acquainted. There remains a natural and perfectly well understood 'qualification' for

57

any one person who is a potential newcomer to the group, namely that he comes from the area speaking the same dialect and sharing the same neighbouring network closely integrated with local agriculture and industry.

Alternatively, in an urban setting where, for example, a person is employed by a large company, his first category people would be his co-workers in the same section or division or in the same factory building. Included in the second category would be all other employees and the management, resulting in a total of, perhaps, 10,000 people or more. In the second category would also come the individual's schoolfriends and fellow university graduates; and if he had kept up a relationship with his friends and contacts who come from his rural background these people would be included too. Finally, there could well be a selection of other people within this group that an individual has come to know through wider business or social contacts.

In certain rural areas, third category people are known as *seken no hito* (others, outsiders, the general public). Overall, the basis for these three divisions in interpersonal relationships is a fundamental and well defined difference in style, approach and manners.

In the first category, as one might well imagine, the style of inter-communication is rather informal. Everybody assumes that they are well informed so that interaction amongst the group becomes more direct and people are more emotionally involved. Use of polite, honorific terms is minimal although there remain various fine nuances for expressing the relative 'closeness' of any one relationship. Generally speaking, there are two basic principles to be applied when using honorific terminology. One covers all honorific forms used by inferiors to superiors; the other applies to more distant relationships when far more honorific forms are used. For example, a senior man both in age and status would use the honorific to a junior man who is not part of the senior man's first category. Logically, therefore, the honorific is used far more extensively within the second category.

Probing more deeply into these three groups or categories one can discover a very obvious and natural basis for what must, in western eyes, appear a very complex form of sociological recognition, in some ways, perhaps, comparable to the different categories within what is called 'British' for the native English, although it is much smaller in scale and within the same culture.

Clearly, it is around the men of an individual's first category that his real sociological importance — his status — revolves. He knows that they (usually his co-workers) are the people with whom he is going to spend the rest of his life; and his reputation and standing will emerge as the result of an accumulation of behavioural responses and contacts between himself and his co-workers. Herein lies the real context of his sociological well-being and he recognizes that the proper functioning of the group and himself within it is his own best form of both personal and emotional security. Naturally, therefore, he takes great care to behave properly, feeling a personal responsibility towards his co-workers, yet at the same time feeling and having considerable latitude to behave freely and to go about his business in the best way he knows how in order to accomplish his objectives. There will even be times when the group will allow him to indulge his own mood and feelings as a child would in a family. Herein lies one of the reasons why Japanese rarely have to rely on professional psychiatrists to help solve personal problems, unlike many western nations.

Within his own group an individual can always find another person with the right sensitivity and understanding to help talk through his personal problems. It can also happen that an individual's predicament or personal behaviour will not be immediately appreciated by the person he is discussing it with; yet, invariably, there will always be someone else in the group capable of grasping the essence of the

Plate 9: *Japanese shyness with foreigners — an impression by artist Michael Foreman.*

Plate 10: *Baseball — one of Japan's leading sports.*

problem and who will take it upon himself to defend the individual concerned and explain his behaviour to the others.

Day to day dealings among one another assume the simplest of forms which certainly help the swiftness and accuracy of communication. Even so, these relationships can be quite demanding on any one individual or group of individuals since one comes to expect a very high degree of sensitivity and understanding from all the others in the group. At the same time, one learns to deal with those whom one does not like very much — simply by developing a certain wisdom in deciding when to make concessions. However, when the 'concessions' limit, as it were, has been reached, a relationship can easily disintegrate and result in quarrels and, occasionally, in a marked hostility which can last for a very long time. When this kind of situation occurs, hostile feelings can be engendered among other members of the same group. Clearly, because of the natural closeness and intimacy prevalent in this first category, it is the one context where you are going to locate your worst enemy.

By contrast, the approach to interpersonal relationships in the second category is rather more formal and is certainly less likely to engender hostile feelings at any time. Traditional Japanese manners and etiquette — the universally appreciated elements of Japanese society — fall within the terms of reference of the second category. The various forms of greeting, referred to earlier, also belong to this category.

When in a situation involving second category behaviour, one becomes more self-restrained yet, at the same time, feeling a kind of affinity and closeness to the other members especially when in the presence of third category people. An almost indefinite number of people can belong to one's second category — people whom one does not know personally but with whom one could become known should it be necessary. When two people come to realise that they belong to this category they automatically feel a certain affinity for and trust in each other even though they have never seen each other before in their lives; instinctively, both parties will realise that they autmoatically have a basis on which to pursue a business transaction or whatever.

Occasionally I am asked, for example, by a professor whom I have never met before — from another faculty of the University of Tokyo — if I would accept a request to give a lecture to a group of his friends. Although he may be my senior in age, he addresses me in the most distinguished honorific terms and says, apologetically, that his friend asked him because he works at the same university as myself. On these occasions, I, as a Japanese, feel quite well disposed to the request and approach it with a certain spontaneous understanding — certainly more so than if I had been asked directly by someone with whom I had no connections at all (i.e. outside my second category). Having a connection makes it more difficult for me to refuse the request.

On another occasion I went to give a series of lectures at a provincial university. As soon as I entered the Faculty of Letters building, I happened to meet one of the faculty professors. He greeted me in a most polite and welcoming way — obviously expecting my arrival. His first words were 'You must be Professor Nakane. I am also from Tokyo; please come and join me in my office'. In his office he offered me tea and began chatting as if he had known me for some time. The fact that he had introduced himself by informing me that 'I am also from Tokyo' left me momentarily puzzled. But I soon realized that his reference to Tokyo meant that he had graduated from the University of Tokyo and not that he came from the city or was born there. In so saying, therefore, he was also informing me of the fact that he belonged to my second category group.

Thus, people of the second category can be approached and are approachable without any need for official introductions. Japanese people are said to be very shy, but, in fact, they are perfectly sociable and enjoy socializing provided they adhere to the correct code of politeness appropriate to this category. Those in this category will

Plate 11: *Graduate students posing for the standard class group picture in the grounds of the local temple.*

naturally seek to impress the others and indicate what fine fellows they are (or could be) since it could well be that either then or at some future date one might want to enter into some form of business dealings. Second category people always feel safer utilizing an existing relationship for approaching another man rather than making a character/suitability judgement for themselves.

There is no doubt that for a Japanese man his sociological world rarely extends beyond this second category. Typically, he would view men of the third category as strangers with whom he has nothing in common.

As a total concept, a Japanese sees society in this way: *ego* with his family (co-residential members) located at the centre which is encircled by men of the first category with the second category forming an outer circle. Beyond that circle there is an indefinite and indefinable world for which he does not even feel it appropriate to apply a particular code of etiquette. In a sense, he is reluctant to have to communicate with this world and within himself he recognizes a certain innate hostility towards it. What is more, he will rarely greet a stranger (who represents this world) even though he may happen to be in close proximity with him such as sitting together at a table in a crowded restaurant.

A person of the third category rarely succeeds in becoming a member of the second or first categories, especially once he has passed his middle twenties. Even if you meet a man of the third category at a party or through a friend (assuming the meeting didn't result in any kind of business dealings), he tends to remain a man of the third category, despite the fact that you will remember his face and name. To see this aspect of the sociological structure being applied one should study Japanese people at, say, a Rotary Club luncheon, where only those who are in the first or second category speak to each other; the men of the third category are virtually ignored even though they are sharing the same table. In these situations first and second category men make no attempt to try and create a relationship with fellow members who belong to the third category, partly because they just don't know what kind of etiquette to apply to a stranger. Either through shyness or simply because they have not the inclination to do so, first and second category men rarely develop a friendship with people of the third category.

The same phenomenon can also be seen at an academic convention where scholars from different universities are assembled together including participants from the third category. At best, the latter will restrict themselves to speaking and putting formal questions at the regular meetings; but they would be most reluctant to talk individually, say, at a casual meeting over coffee. I recall the reaction of certain participants after I had read a paper at an international congress held in Europe. To my great surprise, as soon as the meeting was over, several scholars from different countries approached me with a number of questions and observations concerning my research; some of them even extended an invitation to me to join them for lunch or dinner. Such a spontaneous reaction could never take place in Japan; it would only be one's friends and colleagues who would come forward with comments and remarks after the meeting. It also came as a great surprise to me to see Americans and other westerners eager to become acquainted with people from what I call the third category, and always done in a most pleasant and agreeable manner. Unfortunately, this custom does not exist in Japanese society.

Japanese behaviour depends so much on whether or not there is a specific relationship involved. Correct behaviour patterns will be invariably applied if some form of relationship exists, even if it is only of a temporary nature — providing, of course, both parties realise that some form of mutual involvement (business or whatever) is to follow. This form of temporary or transitory relationship does include third category people, such as shopkeepers and taxi drivers. But except for this kind of incidental 'business' transaction, the average Japanese will feel highly uncomfortable if he has to face a man of the third category. Normally, this discomfort will result in his remaining silent in the hope that he will thereby escape from the predicament as soon as possible; alternatively, he may choose to be rude to achieve the same end. What is sometimes seen as excessive kindness to foreigners combined with a certain form of 'unusual' behaviour is all part of this third category situation. The Japanese do not have an established pattern of behaviour to be applied to those outside their sociological world; nor do they have a universal code of behaviour which is applicable to anyone.

This same sociological concept is obviously closely allied to the problem of mixing with local inhabitants whenever a Japanese travels abroad. In these circumstances it is not unusual for a Japanese to adopt rather aggressive business tactics and remain isolated (at least initially) from the people around him. This kind of behaviour, together with the fact that Japanese stick together in exclusive groups, is considered by many people outside Japan as an expression of Japanese nationalism. In my view, the concept of 'nationalism', of being Japanese' — as understood by a Japanese — is restricted to the level of a simple 'feeling'. In sociological terms they do not consider themselves in relation to other peoples. Their sociological map is ego-centred rather than ethno-centred. In their subjective analysis, even the Japanese themselves, who are in the third category, are treated just like foreigners. The third category people are not seen to be 'different' so much as being 'outsiders'. The Japanese do not see any kind of objective map of society where there are various groups of the same nature, A, B, C, etc, and in which their own group is classified. For a Japanese, different kinds of people are perceived by a different degree of distance from the *ego*, or from the apex of the hierarchical grading order.

This particular Japanese sociological concept seems closely related to their world view of thinking. For example, traditional Japanese concepts do not include the western idea of 'pairs of opposition' (or the structural principle of the distinctive opposition).

Japanese interaction between individuals and between groups tends to be submission by the stronger and adjustment by the weaker, rather than through the coalition or cooperation of equals.

Team spirit *by Anthony Lawrence*

When I watch groups of Japanese tourists abroad, away from their own country, then there seems some truth in the widely-held notion of Japan as a vast, regimented community of hardworking conformists. These groups, marching in tightly-packed formation behind the man with the flag, going where they are told, keeping to the programme — that's very much in keeping with an outsider's idea of the Japanese character. Even when a free afternoon is scheduled in the programme at the end of the visit, say, to Hong Kong, Bangkok or elsewhere, the Japanese tourists don't seem to know what to do with the free time available. They sit in the waiting-room of the local Japanese embassy or consulate until it's time to pack — just to have a taste of home territory, so to speak.

Wherever they are, whether at home or abroad, it is a fact that Japanese people, generally, do not like to behave in an unusual or specially noticeable way. For one thing, they dread the prospect of being thought ridiculous. They have a saying about the nail that sticks out being banged down flat — and it really does apply.

The best time I remember for seeing Japanese men looking most relaxed is when a group of them go to stay at one of Japan's hot-spring resorts, and they stroll through the village all wearing the same kind of comfortable loose-sleeved, *kimono*-type jacket provided by the hotel, with the hotel's name on the back.

Of course, with a nation of over a hundred million people it is very unwise to labour the generalizations. You can talk to many different people and they are likely to react in quite different ways, depending on their place in society, their age bracket, and the amount of exposure they have had to the world outside.

But all of them do have this sense of differentness from the rest of the world — something to do with living on islands. Long conversations with Japanese, whether they are officials, journalists, or housewives, leave an impression of strong, insular, group traditions.

Pride in their country, loyalty, observance of rules of correct behaviour — these are strong factors in the lives of most Japanese. The post-war history of Japan — the low posture during the American occupation, the recovery and extension of Japanese industry and salesmanship burgeoning into the great economic miracle — all that has been made possible by a readiness, on the part of the ordinary Japanese, to work hard and intelligently for modest rewards, as part of a team, in a great project of national reconstruction which he's felt to be a 100 per cent worth the effort and sacrifices involved. Clearly, in joining in this effort his group membership (first in the smaller group of the factory or undertaking, merged, secondly, in the greater group of his country, Japan) has been emphasized and made use of. Why shouldn't he join in a morning song with all the other workers before beginning the day's work in the factory? Why shouldn't the firm play a great semi-paternal rôle in his life? If you are putting the group before the individual, these things follow naturally.

Even so, Japanese people are intensely, humanly aware — and increasingly so — of their changing surroundings. Even among established, middle-aged people observance of agreed rules of public behaviour is by no means blind and unthinking. Japanese men I've met have felt just as much resentment against narrow-minded bureaucrats or inhuman big business as people do in any other sophisticated country. You hear this complaint about traffic congestion in the big cities — 'There isn't even one road with enough walking space for you to walk side by side with a friend to enjoy a conversation'. There is also a growing popular feeling against pollution from factories, with the authorities beginning to take action.

And you meet more men these days with a resentment towards the soullessness of modern life. 'Sometimes I feel that I will have to break loose,' said a quite high-level business executive. 'One day I will leave home in the morning and just disappear and never come back.'

That's a rare attitude, but it exists side by side with the much more common approach of the man on the escalator to success who has no intention of giving up his steadily ascending position. You meet these younger executives in many countries — dedicated, aggressive men, intensely loyal to the firm that has sent them.

Attitudes differ according to age. If you want to learn anything worth knowing about Japan, you have to spend a great deal of time talking to students — not the minority of extremists but the serious young men and women who think about their country and modern society, and look ahead to the kind of lives they want to lead after graduating.

Among many of these young people, there is a growing curiosity about the world outside and the rôle Japan may be playing in it; and keen concern with the new kind of society that will inherit the Japan of today. Sometimes there's doubt and questioning. A young man said to me: 'I am the son of a diplomat. I went to the right school and now I'm at the right university. With my background, I suppose nothing can stop me from becoming an ambassador in thirty years from now. Yet I'm not too happy at the idea of such a settled future. It's better for a man to face more challenges.'

The individual is now becoming more important in Japan. Group psychology — the comfortableness men and women feel when they act in a group — has always been and is still a very powerful force. It could be of enormous importance if national interests were thought to be at stake, if national security were threatened. But in the climate of the present when Japan is the third economically most powerful country in the world, and communications between Japan and other nations are being extended all the time, group psychology is bound to have a diminishing influence on the daily life of Japanese.

People in Japan still do things in large crowds, but often nowadays that's because they have no choice. They live in packed cities concentrated largely in one strip only eighty miles long down the coast of Honshu Island. In recent years there has been more emphasis on leisure; workers are given more free time, more holidays. But where and how to spend the leisure hours and days? Beaches so packed that you can hardly make your way into the sea for a bathe; trains leaving Tokyo so crowded with skiers bound for the hills that the weekends produce their own acute rush-hour situations; fantastic traffic hold-ups on the roads.

Is this because Japanese people always want to do the same thing at the same time? Certainly, in Japan, people like to take their holidays at roughly the same time of year; but that is common to many countries. The real reason for the enormous holiday crushes is that society has provided the leisure time without providing the variety of means and localities for enjoying it in comfort. And yet throughout the country only one out of five Japanese takes all of his paid leave, and 40 per cent use up only half or less. It has even been suggested that if the leisure situation doesn't become more enjoyable soon, more and more Japanese will go back to what they like doing most — work.

Indeed, it seems that there are two powerful elements at work in the Japanese mentality. First, there are the great motivating forces at the basis of Japanese tradition: feelings of obligation and occasionally guilt, feelings of loyalty towards parents, teachers, employers, the emperor and the country. These feelings are still very strong today, among young and old alike. You will meet younger people, of course, who say they have broken free, but they have found nothing with which to replace the old standards; they will conform later. Traditional values obviously have a profound effect on Japanese psychology; when the authorities make any appeal or initiate legislation which brings traditional feelings into play, the response is immediate — as was the case with the Tokyo Olympics and Expo '70 at Osaka. Along with this go certain Japanese characteristics which seem not to have changed over a century — a deep feeling of their separateness, as an island people, from the rest of the world; a keen awareness of other countries, especially western countries, and the possibility of benefiting from western ideas and techniques in furthering Japan's best interests. This homogeneity of outlook — and Japan is a very unified country, very literate, with almost no minority problems of any importance — gives the impression to the outsider of a mass society, with everyone thinking alike. A few years of personal contact with Japan will show that this conception is only partly valid.

The other force at work in Japan is that generated by the nation's own energy in building up an impressive, dominating edifice of industry and export — the urbanization of cities like Tokyo and Osaka, the crowding of millions of people into a density ratio unknown in Europe, and all the transport and pollution problems that inevitably follow. This force of urbanization and factory life might be expected to produce all the more depressing features of group psychology, mass thinking, big city aimlessness and crime problems. But ii does not work out like this with the Japanese. They resist mental pollution. In Tokyo, for instance, the biggest city in the world (outside of China), street crime and vandalism are almost unknown. This despite the fact that television is supposed to have the effect of encouraging crime among the young, and the Japanese are the keenest television watchers in the world. There is a crime problem in Japan, however, and the authorities are worried about it. But the crime figures are far below those of western cities. You can walk anywhere at night in the streets of Tokyo and Osaka without fear of attack.

It is the very conservatism of Japan, its traditionalist view of obligation and behaviour, that today cause its people to question and resist the most recent effects of industrialization.

There are other reasons, too. The time of effort and self-denial for the sake of building up the nation is now seen to be gradually merging into a new historical era, in which big business is no longer automatically identified with the best interests of Japan. For several years now there has been a growing feeling that the welfare of the whole community must be considered. More attention, and money, for example, must be given to create better housing, better hospitals, improved transport, modern drainage. The authorities are very well aware of this pressure; they have increased wages and salaries and they have provided leisure; but the social services are lagging too far behind, and something has got to be done about it.

All this means that the Japanese man in the street has become more important. The individual counts for more than ever before in Japan's history. And increasingly, in the months and years ahead, individual voices will be heard commenting and criticizing. Some of them will be women's voices. The rôle of women in public life is growing all the time — not so much in business, but in medicine, journalism, politics and the civil service. It is not a question of women's liberation — the Japanese woman's role as wife and mother still remains essential to the whole social fabric — but the influence she already exerts indirectly will become more apparent.

None of this means that Japanese national characteristics are undergoing a sweeping change. If the Japanese at home in his own country no longer appears as one face in a row of similar faces, as one smilingly conforming tax-payer among a million, that doesn't mean he's becoming less Japanese, more of a world citizen. A hundred-and-ten million people living on islands with all this history and achievement behind them, who keep talking about *ware-ware Nihonjin* ('We Japanese') — obviously such people have a keen sense of national identity.

It used to be thought, until quite recently, that the Second World War and the American occupation had brought about enormous changes in Japan and Japanese thinking, that links with the traditional past were broken for ever, that henceforth Japan would develop on much more western lines.

But now it seems that, as before, Japan takes from the outside world and adapts it to her purposes, while remaining largely unaffected by outside influences. Japan has absorbed western technology on a tremendous scale, and often improved it to suit her own needs, her own programme of material reconstruction and progress; but that has not changed Japanese basic concepts. Of course the psychology of Japanese society is changing and will change — but it will be in line with Japanese ways and traditions, not in the imitation of foreigners. And despite the anxieties and questionings of the individual, the idea of the group will always remain powerful.

Humour and the Japanese

by Kenichi Yoshida

One does not need to have a sense of humour to laugh. A story once circulated in the days before the war that Ribbentrop, then German Ambassador to the Court of St James, told an English acquaintance of his that when the Führer and his companions, including of course Ribbentrop himself, gathered together and found some matter to laugh over they could not contain themselves and began rolling about on the floor gasping for breath in that eyrie in Berchtesgaden; this is to prove that the Germans too, had a sense of humour. We would not consider either Ribbentrop or the Führer as representing the German people; but it just shows what can be done without a sense of humour, or a sense of anything at all.

Not that we can do without this inestimable gift of seeing a fourth corner in a triangle, as someone put it in describing E. M. Forster's approach to the world; as when he thinks of the map of the United States as a colourful bandanna stretched decorously across the opulent breast of the continent of North America. Humour is something we find we cannot do without when it comes to oiling the rusty and clumsy mechanism of living; without which corrective we should feel ourselves moved at every turn to righteous indignation or maudlin self-pity, or a Job-like refusal to admit the right of anything to exist in the way it does.

The comedy of things tickles us before we begin to moan or curse; or stops us midway and so enables us to save our breath. But the mechanism of living differs according to the locality and the traditional milieu in which it functions; a fact which gives a sort of geographical and historical colouring to the kinds of humour that exist — and so we have Japanese humour and French and American humour, and probably even German humour.

One finds that the difference between pessimism and optimism consists largely in the degree to which one feels oneself prepared to go along with either. At least, we Japanese would seem always to have thought that the ends meet. If a pessimist carries his observations to their logical conclusion and comes to regard the world as an empty show the world becomes just that; even a pessimist has to admit a fact when his convictions confront him with one and the stronger the convictions the more adamant the fact: no room for recriminations or even for feeling pessimistic about it then. But the emptiness of the show does not prevent the world and what he himself does in it from providing him with practically the same reflexes as when he thought the world otherwise; alcohol still inebriates, humour still tickles; he finds himself in a condition differing very little from that of the optimist who has carried his own way of looking at things to its logical conclusion.

For the bare facts of existence do not allow even the optimist to believe that it is roses, roses all the way; he takes the rose for what it is and likes it, knowing quite well that its charm comes as much from the charm being so short-lived as from anything else. He believes, no doubt, in happiness which as far as he himself is concerned ends with him. He may think that it is for the best in the best of all possible worlds; it adds no more to his happiness than to the length of his own existence; nor does it lessen his

Cartoonist, Kon Shimizu, offers his own impression of the author, Kenichi Yoshida

misery when he has toothache. We might say that the optimist is happier personally than the pessimist who feels himself no worse off for differing from the optimist in this slight matter of the fundamental view of things. With the confirmed pessimist and the thorough-going optimist the difference popularly attributed to them ceases to operate.

The Japanese sense of humour would seem to spring from such recognition of popular error. Since we have already seen that laughter has little to do with a sense of humour, the fact that we Japanese laugh a great deal does not teach anyone much about humour — Japanese-style. As a matter of fact, someone has distinguished seven different varieties of Japanese laughter (it may even have been eight, or nine), none of which have anything to do with a person or persons thinking something funny; all the varieties deal with different confused social situations requiring someone to intervene to smooth things out.

The problem before us, therefore, consists in finding out what it is that makes the Japanese laugh — not just to satisfy social etiquette but really laugh. One cannot help thinking of the genuine Japanese laughter as something subdued; not the rollicking laughter of the Cossacks in Gogol, the Rabelaisian kind that rang through that Gargantuan abbey; the sort that has its roots, if one were mean enough to look for such things, in the idea that life lasts for ever and the merriment with it. One may have heard such laughter in the earlier stages of Japanese history. Our warriors of the twelfth and thirteenth centuries seem to have laughed a great deal, boisterous laughter shared by their women; but by that time our history had lasted just so many number of centuries and no race of people can go on being Rabelaisian for ever. Either the race disappears or it matures. A process of maturing over the following seven or eight centuries may have shaped the kind of Japanese humour we know today. One can learn from disillusionment and discover that it amounts to no more than coming to see things as they are.

Growing old should not be synonymous with becoming decrepit — to the point where one can no longer see how funny things are. Life provides any number of examples of incongruity and ineptness; imagine, for example, the richly comic impact of a person who, through his delusions of self-grandeur, presents the appearance of a hippopotamus attempting to do the fan dance. In fact, there is the entire gamut of human folly to consider. Such folly has a history as old as humanity itself and so can grow no older than humanity and Japanese humour, too, finds in it a perennial source of delight.

All that talk we hear about Zen and *haiku* gives quite the wrong impression. On the contrary, half our literature consists of comedy and comic stories having for their material the kind of situations that life abounds in. One might say that humour in that sense has its thread running throughout our history since we find it in our mythology, our earliest recorded and extant novel and the first official collection of our poetry. Later, it developed into various indigenous genres that do not appear to have any counterparts elsewhere. Of these (and here there is no cause to venture into scholarship to discuss Japanese humour), let us examine one example, and let's call it the art of story-telling — which happens to belong rather more to our daily mode of living and life in general than to literature proper. The truth is, most serious students of our literature dismiss this particular genre as 'mere story-telling'. We may call it that, so long as we refrain from putting too much stress on its being that and nothing more. After all, we cannot deny the fact that if we have a funny story to tell it is thanks to the texts which have been handed down from generation to generation.

The corpus of these texts really constitutes a treasure-house of Japanese humour. The popularity of these stories today, in spite of some of them being two or three centuries old, should go to prove that the nature of Japanese humour has remained constant over that period; or should we rather say that the perennially human does not age? But that comes to no more than a truism applicable to all classics and that is what these stories are. Most of them deal with the Japanese way of life which reached a certain peak of perfection during the three hundred years preceding what is usually known as our 'opening up the country' — to western influence and worse (i.e. prior to 1868). I should point out another characteristic of these stories which resides in their dealing exclusively with the life of the common people in their every day town and country setting. There is nothing extraordinary about any of the stories, which brings home to us in its full force the plain truth that we do not have to look far to find material for laughter. The characters that appear in them might be any of us; the things that happen to them have so often happened to ourselves that we have become quite familiar with them beneath the superficial difference in customs, costume and habitat; superficial because in spite of the change in the words we use for our customs and the ferro-concrete horrors we have erected round us, a civilization rooted in the soil like ours only changes with the soil itself. But this sounds like vainglory. One should rather stress the point that Japanese humour delights in the familiar, of the sort that throws light on the mechanism of living.

But like good drama which has to be seen acted for real enjoyment, these stories have to be recounted by professional artists, rather than read privately in scholarly texts. The stories and the art of telling them have developed side by side; the polish which both forms reflect today points to a continuous demand for a good laugh. Any gifted talker, however, should be able to tell a good story; the idea of training and paying men for the purpose may cause some surprise. But a race of people may surely exist that enjoys a good laugh to such an extent that the laughs have to become better and better. This has happened, at any rate, with the Japanese. And so gifted talkers had to look to the quality of their talking. This brings us to the question of subtlety. Here, I have to confess to the terrible truth that a certain amount of subtlety does exist in the Japanese approach to life which no amount of antics on the part of my compatriots abroad may quite suffice to obliterate. One might even explain the crudity of some of these people as an inverted form of subtlety that has lost its bearings. After all, the Japanese race figures among the oldest in the world. Some refinement in the corporate mental make-up should strike anyone as inevitable; and if it affects the racial sense of humour as well, in that case the sense gains instead of losing by it. One may see a damning proof of the truth of this in the fact that so often we hesitate to laugh over a western joke because having understood its message we are left in doubt as to whether that was all that was meant. To put it crudely, for us, so many western jokes lack the final twist that makes a joke seem like a joke.

A look into a room anywhere in Japan where good story-telling is in progress should be a reassuring experience for any western visitor. Apart from the question of intrinsic subtlety, the subtleties or crudities of the language structure might preclude the westerner from any participatory enjoyment of the proceedings. But the laughter itself, hopefully, will strike him as genuine; and if it could be described as rollicking and Rabelaisian, let the visitor reflect on the fact that extreme mirth, engendered in whatever manner, always has this rare quality of making people think that life lasts for ever and the merriment with it.

Japanese shyness with foreigners *by Jun Eto*

A newcomer to Japan might well be surprised to discover that younger Japanese people (say, those under forty) are supposed to have some knowledge of the English language. At junior high school, which is the final stage of the compulsory educational system in Japan, English is taught for three consecutive years. And again at senior high school, students follow English courses for a further three years. This emphasis on English studies is mainly because English is a prerequisite subject of college entrance examinations. Thus, since more than ninety per cent of junior high graduates now go to senior high school in most parts of the country, it follows that approximately ninety per cent of the younger population in Japan is more or less exposed to the English language for a total of at least six years.

However, there is precious little in these facts which will bring any consolation to the foreign visitor. In fact the visitor to Japan will immediately find it very hard to make himself understood to the man in the street no matter where he goes. It is even likely that people will just hold back or run away whenever a foreigner attempts to speak to them.

One day at a Ginza department store, I happened to glimpse an elderly American lady trying desperately to talk to some young sales-girls without apparently any success. The girls shrank back at the sight of a western lady and began whispering hesitantly with one another:

'What shall we do? She's an American lady.'

'Is there anybody who can speak English?'

'You must speak, Haruko. Why don't you take care of her?'

'Me? I can't do that. Let's ask the manager to find somebody who knows how to deal with foreigners.'

But there was no sign of that *somebody* appearing. The American lady, meanwhile, stood there helpless — her eyes looking round as if appealing for assistance. So I decided to volunteer as an interpreter, for I knew all too well how *she* felt and how *they* felt. Incidentally, the girls turned out to be very helpful and courteous once the communication gap was bridged by a passer-by and the American lady continued on her shopping expedition — delighted.

Why, then, did the girls shrink back and appear so reluctant to help their customer from abroad? Obviously, they had no wish to be unfriendly because they were only too pleased to take care of the American lady once they realized that they, too, were able to communicate with her through an interpreter. And, as I indicated earlier, it is also clear that the girls had some knowledge of English since Japanese department stores only hire girls with senior high school education. So, why were they so shy? The answer must point to a psychological problem.

In order to analyse the state of mind of the Japanese when spoken to by an English-speaking foreigner, it is important to understand the meaning of the Japanese word *hazukashii*, which is a difficult word to translate. Literally, it means something like 'to be ashamed of' or 'shy'; but, in fact, it can cover much broader shades of meaning. For example, when one is exposed to unusual circumstances rather suddenly and unexpectedly, one is supposed to feel *hazukashii*. In the same vein, when one finds it difficult to conduct oneself properly, especially in public, one usually feels *hazukashii*. On these occasions, one is apt to say *Ana ga attara hairi tai*, which means 'I wish I could hide myself in a cave'.

Thus, the reason why the girl behind the counter did not attempt to speak to the American lady was that she felt *hazukashii* and, as a result, felt the need to hide herself among the other members of her group who, like her, could barely understand or speak English either. She felt *hazukashii* towards the American lady and towards her friends because she had been singled out from the group and forced into a situation where she had to use a foreign language.

You could say that the reason why none of the girls wanted to speak English was not so much because of their poor knowledge of the language as from an unwillingness to be exposed to a situation in which they would be regarded as different from their friends. The problem is not simply one of linguistic ability. Its roots go down to the deeper stratum of intellectual response.

Here, it is perhaps also necessary to draw attention to the fact that the Japanese do not really lay emphasis upon language as a means of communication. The Japanese are one of the few homogeneous peoples of the world and have contained this homogenic quality for at least a thousand years. Because of this, there is a tacit assumption in their lives that other people are basically an extension of one's self, unlike the peoples of Europe and the West generally where a heterogeneous racial composition is the norm.

In other words, whereas westerners base their lives on the premise that others naturally feel differently about things and view things according to different principles, the Japanese take it for granted in their daily lives that other people (meaning here other Japanese) feel and think the way they do themselves.

It is inevitable, therefore, that the rôle which language plays in communication should decline in such homogeneous surroundings. If others feel and think as one does oneself, the need for explanations almost disappears. Such proverbs as 'The eyes speak louder than the mouth', which state the superiority of non-verbal communication, are by no means rare in Japanese. The Japanese are able to guess at each other's feelings from facial expressions, movements of the eyes and the slightest gestures, and their conjectures are not mistaken.

What happens when a Japanese comes face to face with a completely different kind of person? The literal translation of the phrase which Japanese used to describe westerners in the Tokugawa period is 'red aliens with blue eyes'. Even today foreigners are described in everyday language as *gaijin* (outsiders) or *gaijin-san* (literally, Mr Outsider). How, then, does a Japanese feel when he is suddenly confronted with a *gaijin* who speaks to him?

For a start he, the Japanese, is bound to feel that he has no opportunity of applying the non-verbal communication at which he is so proficient. Here is a case in which eyes do not 'speak louder than the mouth' since the colour of the foreigner's eyes is different. As an aside I would say that there is a strong tendency for Japanese people to think that all foreigners have blue eyes; it does not matter that your eyes may, in fact, be brown or black. The reason for this is that, when a Japanese is addressed by a foreigner, he is so surprised that he just simply doesn't notice the colour of the other's eyes.

The first reaction, for the Japanese therefore, is one of shock. Remembering that Japanese incline towards non-verbal rather than verbal communication, it is clear that this is a situation in which absolutely no contact is established and that the expressed surprise of the Japanese stems from the fact that a person with eyes and hair of a non-communicative colour should seek to communicate with him.

Moreover, the words the other person is using are foreign. If a Japanese were spoken to in his own language, he could at least reply in that language, but his mind boggles at the fact that he must speak in a foreign language. Instinctively, he feels he must escape — not so much from the *gaijin*, but from the situation itself. Often as not, therefore, he will disappear without answering the question.

The same thing would happen if you were to address him in French or German instead of English. Even if you were to speak to him in strongly accented Japanese he would be convinced, no doubt, that you were talking English. To many Japanese the phrase 'a foreign language' is synonymous with the word 'English'. As a matter of fact, to the average Japanese, anything that a foreigner speaks sounds like English.

One reason for this is the same as that which causes Japanese people to think that all westerners have blue eyes. Other contributing reasons include the fact that, since the beginning of modernization, the Japanese have been subjected to a strong Anglo-Saxon influence — partly as a result of the old Anglo-Japanese alliance (signed in 1902), and then later through the post-war years of the American occupation.

If you speak to a Japanese in a foreign language, or in such poor Japanese that it sounds like a foreign language, you will probably be taken for an American, because in most cases, the Japanese are unable to distinguish by sight between Americans and Europeans. If you deny that you are an American, it is just possible that a Japanese might get as far as suggesting that you are Canadian, Australian or, perhaps, German, but he will get no farther than that.

The strange thing is that, even if you speak with a typical British accent, only highly educated Japanese who have lived abroad, or whose jobs take them abroad, will be able to identify you as English or 'British'. Sadly, for some reason, the British presence in Japan since the war has noticeably declined. Thus, to the average Japanese, all foreign languages sound like English, and all English sounds like American English.

It is unnecessary for me to add, I think, that even if, because of what I have said up till now you were to speak in an American accent, the situation would not be improved. When a *gaijin* speaks to the Japanese man in the street, the Japanese shrinks back, gives an awkward smile, and then, without a word, disappears into his group as quickly as possible. And, remember, these are people who have learned English for at least six years.

It may be of interest at this point to discover what, and from whom, the Japanese learn during their six years of English education at junior and senior high school.

There is no denying that they all learn English, but they learn it from Japanese teachers. Probably only one in a thousand of these teachers, however, has ever studied in an English-speaking country, or lived abroad. That is to say the teachers have learned their English from Japanese professors at university. Again, I would say that only about one in ten of Japanese professors who teach English or English literature have ever studied in Britain or America and can speak English without strain. Dr Reischauer once said, 'The Japanese who speak the best English are natural scientists. Next come businessmen, then those in the humanities and the social sciences. Right at the end come scholars of English and English literature.'

Unfortunately, this is very much the case. Thus, those who teach English at junior and senior high school became teachers of English, having learned English in Japanese from Japanese professors!

Well, then, what do junior and senior high school pupils learn from these teachers who have themselves learned English in Japanese? It is not English itself, but rather the way to solve a puzzle called 'English'. The reason for this lies in the fact that English, as I have said, is a compulsory subject in university entrance examinations, and the questions on 'English' which are set in these examinations are just like puzzles. Japanese people term this 'English' 'examination English' and, quite rightly, differentiate between it and normal spoken and written English.

Thus, even if at the end of six years of 'English' education some Japanese pupils become proficient in 'examination English', they cannot, of course, write English, let alone speak it, and the end result is that they cannot even read an English newspaper to any satisfactory degree, without the aid of a dictionary and the expenditure of a great deal of time. Only a very few pupils, such as those chosen to spend a year studying in America (under the auspices, say, of the American Field Service), ever gain sufficient linguistic ability to enable them to use English as a means of international communication.

Having considered such a detailed analysis of the problem, readers might feel that things are hopeless — at least for the visitor to Japan wanting to make his way around and to communicate with everyday folk. However, the position is not entirely without hope. For one thing, the number of Japanese who learn English outside the framework of formal school education is rapidly increasing year by year. Japanese people are beginning to realize just how necessary English is for business purposes and are shocked at the inferiority of their own English ability. People who think in this way are, for the most part, very keen on speaking English and tend to improve rapidly.

However much Japanese people may feel *hazukashii* and want to hide, the world is growing smaller, and this requires that Japan recognizes her responsibilities as a member of the international community.

Japan looks into the crystal ball

by Nobutoshi Hagihara

A new field of private enterprise is opening today for imaginative Japanese. It requires scarcely any capital investment, and domestic demand is growing so fast that an energetic person should soon make a fortune. In this case, from telling other people's.

The Japanese seem to have taken to fortune telling in a big way, and customers for the new entrepreneurs include not only those traditional victims of the mountebank — ignorant peasants and flighty young women — but also serious students anxious about their exam results. Such modernity in an ancient trade is altogether welcome: as a mode of reaction against the dominance of the computer, it implies a reversion to human agencies which has much to recommend it. For the computer has in recent years introduced a more primitive mode of behaviour: people in advanced societies today often entrust their romantic, or even their material, future to a computer, whose electronic selection methods they suppose to be more reliable than their own haphazard processes. Compared with that, merely to ask about the future would seem to be positively enlightened. But enlightened though it be, and suitably adapted to modern needs, it is still somewhat surprising to come across such fortune telling in Japan.

Fortune tellers one associates with India, or with the gypsies of Europe. But in China and Japan superstition has traditionally taken more complex forms. Divination might have much the same result, but it is not the same thing; it requires an elaborate education and is a process learned rather than a mysterious gift bestowed. More than that, the ability to divine the future, to determine auspicious and inauspicious times for action and decision, commonly goes with a strong sense of social propriety. Superstition in Japan has indeed amounted to one of the social graces. How else could it have bulked so large in classical literature? The lives of Heian court ladies (early Heian period 794-876 AD) sometimes were dominated by it — by having to wait for their lovers interminable hours or days because the poor fellows had to make impossible journeys to avoid unlucky routes. All quite endurable, or so it

Plate 12: *Fortune teller in Shinjuku, Tokyo.*

Plate 13: *Fruit on display in a shop window.*

78

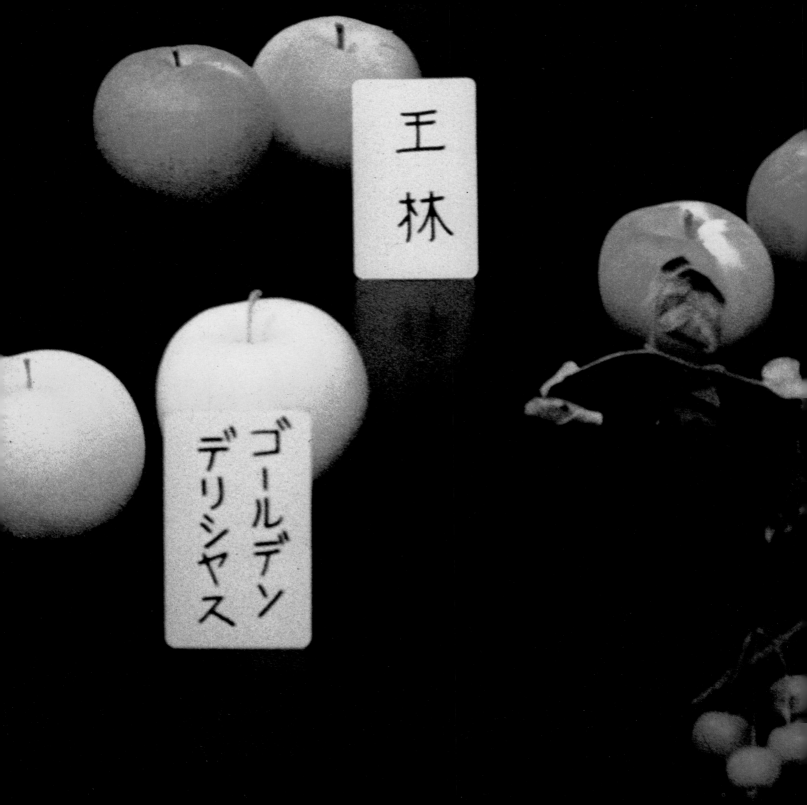

seems, and presumably because superstition was part of the whole social system. And in that sense, perhaps it wasn't superstition at all. Perhaps Japan is only now discovering it.

If everybody believes something — that a certain consequence will follow from such an action, or that such an attitude is right and the other wrong, then it is no longer superstition but belief. Traditionally the Japanese have accepted belief but rejected superstition. Superstition is really a belief that is not socially accepted. And that is why superstition has flourished in Europe but so far failed miserably in Japan. Europe has always said that if the Christian religion is true, then no other can be. There is only one God. There is — or should be — only one Church; and the bloodiest wars until this century were fought to establish whether there could indeed be more than one church at a time. Japan on the other hand has always suggested that different beliefs might be acceptable as true in different contexts. Is there only one Godhead? Then let the eight million divine spirits of the Shinto belief be reckoned *Bodhisattvas* (earthly representatives of Buddha — Buddha incarnate). There indeed is tolerance! Tolerance on a scale that Europe never dreamed of when the philosophers of three centuries ago were elaborating their theories of toleration. And if this tolerance should be thought uncomfortable in the experience of an individual person, well, the Japanese had an answer for that too. It is an old truism in Japan that one is Shinto at birth and Buddhist at death. Most parents would not dream of taking a new-born baby to call on all their ancestors at a Buddhist temple; but most people would be content to say farewell to this world amid the monotonous chanting there.

In between these two experiences, the Japanese in general are pretty irreligious. Obviously there are some who hold deeply to their Buddhist, Shinto, or even Christian beliefs. But the number is very small. For a great majority, religion is more of a pleasure than it is in Europe; that is to say, religious holidays are frequently taken seriously enough to tempt the family into a visit to the temple and an excursion to accompany it, whereas in Europe the religious element is generally ignored altogether. It is still normal in Japan to perform the wedding ceremony according to the Shinto ritual, but even here Christianity is making large inroads. Popular women's magazines carry stories almost every month of how particular young couples were married in such and such a Christian chapel, and the stories seem designed merely to whet the appetite for the advice following: how to have a Christian marriage ceremony without becoming Christian. When the heir of the supreme guardian of the Shinto religion, namely the Crown Prince, was married several years back, nobody seemed the slightest bit perturbed that his wife had received a thoroughly Catholic education from school to college.

So, indifference or enlightenment? Whichever it be, the Japanese have developed an extraordinary all-embracing attitude to religion. Few Japanese biographies would begin with the terrible kinds of childhood that have in the past made so many European lives miserable, dominated as they were by the fear of a vengeful God. But the spirit of tolerance also has its disadvantages. Without anything or anybody as absolute as Almighty God in Christian society, it is difficult to develop a truly independent mind — paradoxical, but true. To be a *self*, one needs someone ultimately indivisible to refer to, and without that, one tends to look for reinforcements for a self in the world around. Which is probably why the Japanese have acquired the reputation of living, breathing and thinking communally. This reputation is undeserved and unjust; but the family, the company, Japan itself, have often been used to fill a gap in one's own relation with oneself that the inheritors of the western tradition are simply not aware of. And outside this, some kind of moral authority has to be found in this world, since the power of the other was never quite determined: if,

Plate 14: *Scene from Kurosawa's* Dodeska-Den *(1970)*.

83

after all, one is quite sure about the absolute power of God, one is that much less concerned with the claims of a Republic or the mystique of a King. But if one is simply rubbing along with eight million or so invisible spirits, the need for some visible authority is rather stronger, and in the past, the Emperor, or the nation, or perhaps for a time America, or even, may the spirits help us, the GNP, have become repositories for such moral claims on our attention. The future of such idols is now harder to see. *Issun-saki wa yami*, as they say in Japan, meaning literally: an inch in front of us all is darkness. But all the same this uncertainty is something the Japanese are used to. They have been through it all before, and in spiritual or mental terms, they have always lived like that. They expect really to be able to carry on, and in this sense, in spite of their reputation, they are probably optimists at the bottom of their hearts. Another proverb puts it rather well: *Kaho wa nete mate*, which means literally that the best way to wait for events to take a better turn is just to keep on quietly sleeping.

Economically and socially, the Japanese are an almost obsessively energetic people. Spiritually, they are a nation of Micawbers — optimistic and indecisive. Their religious tolerance contributes to this, and so do their religious practices — waiting for good days for weddings, or for going into hospital, or avoiding an inauspicious room plan in a house. All this they further augment by a generous rifling of other people's customs, such as the celebration of *Kurisumas* on 25 December each year. But it is all rather passive, a policy of wait and see, an avoidance of all things inauspicious. True European style superstition, on the other hand, demands a quite different mental attitude. In Japan an unlucky direction, an inauspicious day, is unlucky for everybody travelling, inauspicious for everybody getting married. In Europe, one's fortune was one's own, like one's face; but unlike the face it was generally kept hidden from everyone else, secretly told and paid for, changed by unaided individual efforts. And perhaps this is why traditional superstitions have declined in Europe, why fortune telling does not often happen at the fairground in a European town now, but has been replaced by popular astrology in the newspapers. People are losing their sense of individuality and their ability to influence their own fates. Instead, they are becoming more content to think that they might share their fortunes with every other reader of the same newspaper born under the same star.

This is the reason, perhaps, for the increase in fortune telling, for the discovery of superstition in Japan. The social world of the Japanese, on which they once relied to supplement their perhaps too tolerant religious system, has become increasingly uncertain, and so, with undaunted optimism, they are turning to practices which re-emphasize their individuality, are turning to more social forms of superstition. It is an odd situation: it looks as if the two are approaching each other, whereas they are engaged on opposite courses. But it does mean that the Japanese can now enjoy the fortune telling boom.

And the entrepreneurs: what should they do? First, they should not forget some of the old methods of Chinese divination, which make fortune telling more respectable anyway, but have the merit of being Chinese at a moment when China is once again almost an obsession in Japan. Secondly, look old. No one, anywhere, has ever trusted a young fortune teller. So make up if need be. Thirdly, learn more about the beautiful ambiguities of literary Japanese. Whoever trusted a straightforward fortune teller? And by the same token, why has fortune telling not been a Japanese speciality from long ago? Japan has what is probably the world's richest language in ambiguity. And finally, having done all that, make sure that the *yakuza*, the honourable gangsters, don't mind you operating in their locality. In the Ginza, Shinjuku, Shibuya, and Asakusa, in Tokyo, it might be a good idea as in other parts of the world to do more than promise them a good fortune: one might have to share one's own.

84

Youth: the new face of Japan

by Pierre Anger

Anatomy of Dependence, Kodansha, Tokyo, 1973

Japanese children surprise us by their roundness, their freshness, their lion-cub grace. It is well-known that Japan is a paradise for children, a country where they are coddled, carried piggyback and where, from an early age, they share the daily life of the adults. In this sense, the umbilical cord of a Japanese is never cut. Hence his dependence (the concept *amae* on which Professor Takeo Doi lays great emphasis*), but also his precociousness. Specialists confirm that the Japanese child talks earlier than the western child and proves very quickly that he has a gift for mathematics.

So it comes as a great surprise to the western observer to see these young fledglings conform so quickly to the laws of the society at large where they end up accepting more of a caged existence, finding a taste for life in groups and clubs. Again, it is surprising to see how old people in Japan regain their childhood freedom and often end their days in the family group. They become lions again, but their manes are white.

Consequently, the development of the 'homo japonicus' seems to be the exact opposite to that of western man. If one pictures life as a graph with its high and low points, the Japanese graph reveals two high points, two peaks of privileged status; on the one hand childhood and adolescence, on the other hand old-age. The depression of the curve represents adult life. The curve of western life, however, has one high point only, adult life, framed by two depressions. In the East, wisdom is the acceptance of the human and cosmic laws. In the West, one must take the opposite course, fighting against the world, the better to dominate it and prove one's strength.

However, this traditional pattern is changing, both in the East and the West, partly because of the influence of psychology on education. Thus, in Europe and America, an attitude of 'laisser-faire' has been adopted towards children and adolescents identical to that customary in Japan. In Japan, on the other hand, there is a move in the opposite direction, and today we are witnessing the development of a policy for youth. What the Japanese Government wants is the replacement of mass education by quality education. There is no doubt that Japan needs to make greater efforts in the field of fundamental and applied research and so achieve the technological and political emancipation she obviously wants.

This wager on youth and on a planned youth and education policy is in fact a wager on the future, which is perfectly justified when one considers that on 1 October 1973 there were 36,422,000 people under twenty. Statistics also showed that 65 per cent of the population at that time was under forty.

The young people of Japan are not only being changed by their everyday life, but also by the flood of foreign fashions and values. They, in turn, are greatly influencing their environment.

May 30, 1972. Attack on Lod Airport, Israel, by three young Japanese terrorists defending the Palestinian cause. Outcome: 24 dead and 70 wounded. Two terrorists killed, the third serving a sentence in Tel-Aviv prison. This bloody attack taught the whole world that a new phenomenon had crept in among the cars, transistor radios, and oil-tankers labelled 'made in Japan' — the guerilla phenomenon. What is their motivation? In addition to revolutionary convictions, there is certainly an element of romanticism and a taste for the exotic. This desire to escape from Japan as a result of the lack of space, promiscuity and the high cost of living is greatly increasing, but it is Japan's youth who feel the need most strongly, especially if they have already tasted foreign travel.

This 'disorientation' by magnetic storms outside is accompanied by a radical physiological and psychological transformation. Statistics tell us how many kilogrammes or centimetres the young people are putting on each year — so much so that obesity is becoming quite common. And the differences in outlook between the present and past generations can be seen in the increase in cosmetic surgery operations, long hair for young men and short hair for girls, and curled or dyed hair for both, the wearing of beards and moustaches (traditionally abhorred by the Japanese), the taste for jeans, bright colours. . . . But it is in the area of food that the generation gap is at its widest.

When I spent a holiday at Miyakejima (in the south of the Izu peninsula) with my Japanese in-laws, I found that the tastes of my two little nieces, Chieko and Makiko, were completely different from those of their parents and their grandmother. They preferred bread, butter, spaghetti, hamburgers, and the only traditional Japanese foods they liked were those that were similar to western food, such as the *soba* dishes, for example. Again, can you imagine what the first thing was the twenty-four-year-old Japanese solo sailor, Yoaoki, asked for on landing in Australia after a voyage lasting 94 days and covering 41,000 kilometres? A steak and a glass of beer! What would the classical Japanese have asked for in similar circumstances? A bowl of *misochiru* (bean curd soup) or some *chazuke* (rice sprinkled with green tea and seasonings).

Behaviour patterns are also changing. Like most young Japanese, Isoko, my wife, can no longer bear to sit for long with her legs folded under her. Similarly, Japanese politeness, invented primarily for the benefit of the men, faces growing neglect. For example, I recently heard a story about two young secretaries who got out of a lift first instead of giving way to the male occupant: 'Really!', he declared, 'Did you see that? The young people today just don't know how to behave any more!'

The phenomenon of westernization is going even further than one might think. (It corresponds, moreover, to a parallel phenomenon of 'easternization' among young people in the West.) Thus, Bach or Mozart are more Japanese than *gagaku* (classical music of the Imperial court) — so the philosopher Nishitani recently remarked to André Malraux. One might add that, by a similar development, Coca-Cola, whisky or beer are now more Japanese than *sake*.

So much for the evidence. What is increasingly apparent is the fact that there are now two different sides to Japan — the Japan of spartan ways, vegetarian, respectful of tradition, sacrificing body and soul to the group identity, and attached to the sober, the discrete and the neutral (these three epithets are covered by the one word *shibui* in Japanese), and a Japan that is diurnal, colourful, free from complexes, a young Japan that grows as one watches it, cries out loud and kicks.

How then is this conflict going to develop? Is society, and the 'system', still powerful enough to bring back those who stray from the fold? It is difficult to foresee the future, especially when it involves accounting for irrational elements. However, one thing is sure, and that is that Japan has mastered the art of peaceful revolutions.

It is possible that the young people of Japan, who want everything immediately, may provoke the conflagration. Their strength, and at the same time their weakness, is their fighting spirit. Indeed, one of Japan's most enduring values, over the centuries, has been its warrior spirit. Exactly what rôle it will play in today's world remains to be seen.

Zen: a personal encounter

by William MacQuitty

In Japan the harshness of the elements is a fact of life. Typhoons and earthquakes regularly exact their toll. Most of the land is covered by infertile rock and numerous volcanoes sit sometimes in silence, sometimes in anger — a daily reminder of the power of Nature. Yet in spite of these daunting circumstances, the Japanese are able to take advantage of the inevitable and like their oysters turn liabilities into pearls.

The essence of this attitude to life is found in their interest in Zen, which if only actively followed by a minority has a deep hold on the minds and thoughts of most. Introduced to Japan from China under the Hojo government in the thirteenth century, Zen established itself as the most significant refinement of the Buddhist beliefs which first came to Japan via the Asian continent in the middle of the sixth century. According to Daisetz T. Suzuki, acknowledged as the world's leading interpreter of Zen: 'Of all the Buddhist sects or schools, including those developed in Japan such as the Nichiren and the Shin, the Zen sect is to be singled out as a unique spiritual force that has contributed so much to the formation of Japanese culture and character'.

Prior to the sixth century the Japanese had worshipped their ancestors and the forces of nature which were indeed formidable. The advent of Buddhism confronted them with new patterns of thought; compassion came to be reflected in their good manners to each other and to strangers, and this attitude to life was strengthened by a supreme sense of service to their country and to their work.

Thus, largely through the influence of Zen and its search for 'enlightenment' and spiritual 'awakening', the Japanese people have become masters of a simplicity and purity of expression that has rarely been equalled. Their meticulous approach to life stripped away non-essentials and revealed a chastity of taste that forbade all embellishment. This proclaims itself in the lovely interiors of their homes, the elegant but stern lines of their temples, the exact spacing of each stone and tree, each shrub and flower and the pools and waterfalls of their exquisite gardens. Above all the Japanese craftsman and artist knew what to leave out, they knew more than anyone else the use of emptiness and silence. This is seen in the simple lines of everyday objects: the cups and saucers of the 'tea ceremony', the ladle and the teapot are not only delicately beautiful in themselves but part of a graceful way of living and spiritual enrichment. The bowls and containers of wood, the pure lines of the lanterns of papers as well as stone, the practical simplicity of the fresh robe and sandals which await the traveller in every inn, and the appetizing food prepared so that it is as attractive to look at as it is to taste. This simplicity is the keynote to Zen.

Zen may seem difficult to the western mind, but like so many of the good things in Japan it is a philosophy for the meek rather than the sophisticated. The goal is to see one's own nature, to 'know thyself', to break down the bars of the intellect and to let the light flood in. Zen is a sudden act of recognition.

The Zen way of life cannot be learned in a day. Yet as one travels from the pulsating life of Tokyo on the fastest train in the world through empty plains, with Mount Fuji towering in the distance, a feeling of peace invades the spirit. This is strengthened as one descends at Kyoto and reaches its culmination amongst the tranquil temples and gardens which cradle Zen thought. Here in 'The Great Sea' garden of the Daisen-in or the Zen garden of Ryoan-ji it would be hard for even the most insensitive traveller not to pause for a moment's reflection on the secret of life.

Picture sequence: *1. The bell of Tenryu-ji (Temple of the Celestial Dragon) at Kyoto. Tenryu-ji is one of the branches of the Rinzai division of the Zen sect. 2. The tranquillity of water. 3. Solitude and silence in the garden of the fifteenth-century Ryoan-ji temple, Kyoto. It consists of fifteen rocks and a stretch of white sand carefully raked into broad parallel lines. The garden has been described as a 'Zen poem in minerals and light'.*

A sense of belonging

by Shuichi Kato

A striking characteristic of Japanese society is the smoothness with which members of a small group communicate with each other. Equally striking, but in contrast, is the difficulty experienced by members of one group in communicating with members of another group. We could call these forms of communication 'intra-group communication' and 'inter-group communication', respectively. In my view, many problems of understanding that emerge within the context of international dealings are simply a reflection of the basic group structure of Japanese society.

Much has already been said on the subject of Japanese village cooperatives, which have long existed among farming communities. As a broad generalization one could say that the relationship between members of a village is universalistic *(Gemeinschaft)* and not particularistic *(Gesellschaft)*. The members of the co-operatives have a strong sense of belonging to the village, and value the village as a whole over the value of individual members. Although the cooperative's structure included a superior-inferior relationship between members, there is also a marked level of lateral relationships (egalitarianism).

During the time of Emperor Meiji (1868-1912) other small groups (such as business organizations) developed the same kind of village cooperative 'consciousness', but where the system of superior-inferior relationships was greatly stressed.

After the Second World War, however, the particular, and in some cases extreme, emphasis formerly applied to the system of superior-inferior relationships was noticeably modified. (In this sense, I suggest that post-war companies are much closer to the original village cooperative prototype than their pre-war counterparts.) However, the universalistic relationship between members, the strong sense of belonging to a group and the tendency for the group to be superior to the individual did not change. These characteristics, in fact, are very much part of modern-day Japan.

An interesting example is the system of 'lifetime employment', prevalent throughout companies, government offices, and in the field of education, where the overwhelming majority of employees remain with the same employer until retirement. Japan is the only advanced capitalist country in which this system is practised. Typically, the individuals concerned spend their leisure time as members of a group — playing golf, for example, attending parties, playing *mah-jong* and going on trips together. Relationships also develop which involve the whole family: courtesy calls at the beginning and end of the year, exchanging presents during the gift seasons, and acting as go-betweens for marriages. Contact between these people is certainly not confined to the obligatory area of work, but touches every facet of their personalities and life styles.

Since the act of becoming employed means that one has chosen a place of work for life, it closely resembles the act of getting married. Just as the majority of married couples do not divorce so the majority of government officials, teachers and company employees do not change their place of work. And just as the concept of 'one flesh' pertains in marriage, so the idea of complete union with one's office, school or company becomes idealized. Almost inevitably, of course, the company worker is left almost no room to display his individuality outside his place of work.

In addition to 'lifetime employment' there is the system of 'rank according to length of service', which has great advantages for the employee. First, the employee need have no fear of being 'kicked out into the street'. Above all else, lifetime employment guarantees security. Although there is fierce competition for promotion within the group, the results of this competition are not so blatantly apparent or destructive as in western capitalist countries, since the system provides an honourable and well-paid sinecure even for those officials and company workers who drop out of the race.

Things are so arranged that a department head in a company, or the head of a government office, will never be replaced by a young, able section chief, as so often happens in the West (with a resulting loss of honour and income) unless he does something very wrong indeed. Thus, there is no need for a senior person to fear an able junior, or wish to restrain him from showing his ability. Indeed, on the contrary, since the good work of a junior is to the credit of a senior, the senior will encourage his juniors and treat them with parental affection.

It goes without saying that this is also an excellent system from the employer's point of view. A Japanese employer might well agree that a policy which pursued the principle of free-market competition for labour would probably increase the efficiency of his firm, but the smoothness of human relationships within it would undoubtedly be impaired, and, as a result, he could not expect any guarantee of employee loyalty, even if he offered high salaries.

Unanimity within the group is always highly valued. Minority opinion is something that should not really exist; of course, if it does exist it is looked upon as an unfortunate and abnormal situation. Often enough, therefore, the will of a meeting is not decided by a majority vote. (This is as true of political party committee meetings as of village assemblies.) In principle, an individual would usually choose to examine the general trend and quietly follow that, rather than explain and defend a minority viewpoint.

During this sort of meeting any attempt to be explicit in defending an opinion could be quite harmful. It would certainly be considered unnecessary. Not unnaturally, therefore, certain linguistic conventions have evolved which leave opinions unclear and respect other people's feelings. In fact, one could almost say that the ideal communication does not depend on language. It is really a question of telepathy. In years gone by, itinerant *samurai* would draw their swords and attack each other simultaneously after a mere exchange of glances. Similarly, the Chinese Zen monk Rinzai would give a yell of encouragement to a pupil, and the Zen monk Tokuzan would strike a pupil with a stick. Such methods have constituted important forms of intra-group communication between two people who are a small unit within a group. The fighting staves used by students of the Neo-Left Wing are probably not unconnected with the traditions of the Zen Sect which have been passed on from the time of the Kamakura Period (1192-1573). It seems that a strong sense of mistrust always develops when people try to understand each other by means of words.

Intra-group communication in our daily lives depends, to a greater or lesser extent, on telepathy. However, it is not possible to rely on telepathic communication when people outside the group are involved. Moreover, since a small group is exclusive to those outside it, there is a marked tendency for every member to define his relationship with an outsider, not by putting himself in the position of the other person, but by thinking of the relationship between his group and the outsider.

The simplest form of relationship between one's group and another person is either that of a friend or a foe; and, generally speaking, this is how Japanese classify outsiders. When it is a friend, intra-group communication by telepathy is applied. But, since the other person has not shared the experience of living in the same group, he will, obviously, experience some difficulty in understanding group sense and sensitivity.

If an enemy, or a potential enemy is involved, extremely formal words which have no substance are used.

Inevitably, therefore, the use of formal language in the shape of civilities makes the communication of thought content very difficult, sometimes impossible. 'The Japanese,' it is said, 'are the politest people in the world. But they're always laughing, so you can't tell what they're thinking.'

Simply speaking, we have a choice of two completely different attitudes which we can adopt with regard to inter-group communication. The first is an extension of the intra-group system and relies on telepathy or what is commonly called 'communication at gut level'. The custom of inviting people to a party when there are 'difficult' things to discuss probably stems from this. Beyond the simple commercial effectiveness of such a move, there is an implied awareness of the difficulties of inter-group communication and an anticipation of the physio-psychological efficacy of alcohol. (A mistrust of verbal communication.)

The second attitude is the complete antithesis of that seen in intra-group communication, and is a kind of verbal expression which has been ritualized and hollowed out. If the ideal of intra-group communications is substance without words, then it follows that typical inter-group communication is words without substance.

There are, of course, exceptions to this. An important one is purely technical language. Technical language can be understood by anybody, regardless of the type of group to which he belongs. This is as true of Japan, of course, as of any country. However, this does not mean that intra-group (and therefore inter-group) human relations among scientists and technologists differ basically from what I have hitherto said on the subject.

Looked at from the Japanese point of view, contact with foreigners is, for a start, an extreme case of inter-group communication. As a rule, the Japanese will respect the other person's feelings and treat him politely. Since we also fear that our feelings may be hurt (not knowing whether the other person is a friend or an enemy) we become non-committal and pile up polite words — taking our cue from the other person. What's more, we have the pre-conceived belief that 'it is impossible to have a *substantially* meaningful conversation with a foreigner, anyway'.

This reference to 'substance' is a delicate and complex concept. It is connected with the whole of our emotional life. It is difficult to put into words and it can really only exist in topics of an intra-group nature. Any other substance exists purely in technical topics. For example, when a Japanese says 'Do Westerners understand Bassho's poetry?' he is definitely not asking a question. What he means is 'Westerners do not understand Bassho's poetry'. Or he may even mean 'Westerners *must* not understand Bassho's poetry'.

As the relationship progresses, the Japanese may come to realize that the foreigner is not as different as he had first thought. If the foreigner is an Asian, the similarity between his features and build and those of the Japanese will play an important rôle initially. Once the Japanese has categorized the other person as a friend and come to feel closer to him, he will not be able to continue for long with his polite inter-group form of communication. A spectacular change will take place and he will quickly and suddenly change to the telepathic form of intra-group communication.

3 Creative world

Plate 15: *Neon sign in Tokyo.*

Plate 16: *Multi-tier flyover in central Tokyo.*

Plate 17: *The quiet beauty of Japan's unspoiled countryside.*

Plates 18 and 19: *Children from the Suzuki school of music in concert.*

才能教育 第22回夏期学校

Artist and folk pottery in Japan *by Bernard Leach*

Handicrafts in Japan have been fast disappearing throughout this century and only a little remains which is of pure content. This is true of all industrialized countries where the machine from the West is eliminating the use of man's hands as the direct tools of his feeling, intuition and imagination.

During the last century, more precisely from the time of William Morris in England, a revolution, although minor and quiet, has taken place. An attempt was made by artist-craftsmen to preserve some beauty in our daily life. This movement started in Japan in 1929 under the leadership of Dr Soetsu Yanagi, Shoji Hamada and Kanjiro Kawai, who founded the National Folk Arts Society and its museum in Tokyo. It should be borne in mind that this Japanese movement was based upon a Buddhist aesthetic and that therefore its expression was deeply oriental and by no means a mere copy of the West. Yanagi did two things: one was to collect and display in those now many museums the beauty of oriental crafts made mainly by groups of country craftsmen guided by faith and tradition. This was in contrast to work now being made in small quantities by individuals whom we call artist-craftsmen.

Dr Yanagi's second achievement was to give unfailing support to genuine artistry; he had that discriminating vision and insight for what was true and beautiful, inherited from generations of Tea Masters. Since he died in 1962 his work has been carried on with equal perception and leadership by the potter Shoji Hamada. I do not think that my old friend Yanagi seriously thought that he could stave off this great evolutionary change, or preserve handicrafts on a wide scale, but he did keep them alive as far as he and his friends were able to find new markets for country craftsmen, mainly in the cities. This was achieved partly by the publication of magazines, first *Kogei* and then *Mingei*, which during the last forty years or so have bridged a gap between countrymen and townsmen. The less conscious countryman and the more

107

fully conscious artist-craftsman have been better interrelated than in any other country — East or West. Dr Yanagi himself said that the function of the artist-craftsman, though travelled, educated and eclectic, was to pilot entry into a new age. His doctrine was uncompromising, for it stated that the conscious artist could seldom achieve a comparable wild-flower purity. He did say that at the Round Table in his Heaven of Beauty there was no top nor bottom, meaning that there was room for all which is pure by whomsoever produced. There is no escaping the sharp-edged verity of this oriental concept, born of what is called the 'Iron Hammer of Zen'. It strikes equally at so many established reputations, both in the East and in the West; in fact, is not this a concept to which most of us would subscribe?

We are living in a period which the English historian, Arnold Toynbee, has written of as a time which in the future will mainly be regarded as the beginning of deep understanding and interplay between the two world hemispheres. The ranks close, the world shrinks. This scientific age has brought fast and sudden means of communication so that the young as never before inherit the earth — all beliefs, all cultures, all artifacts.

Pilgrims in Japan used to walk its many and mountainous miles carrying on their hats those Buddhist words:

There is no East,
There is no West,
Where then the North and South?

A broader sketch of the general position seemed necessary before drawing attention to those qualities which are unique in Japanese pottery — undoubtedly best expressed by the adjective *shibui* or by its noun *shibusa*, which have no English equivalent. In Japan these are words used and accepted by everyone as denoting the essence of Buddhist beauty — nobility combined with humility — naturalness with the greatest refinement. The root of these words is *shibu*, which is the astringent juice of the persimmon tree. Thus Dr Yanagi compared the quality of *shibusa* with holy poverty, which is more of the heart than of austerity.

With this thought and yet one other, namely *kisu*, or irregularity — 3-5-7 etc instead of 2-4-6 etc — one finds the keys to the Japanese sense of beauty, particularly in pots — in shape, colour, texture and pattern. These are Buddhist concepts indicating man at one with nature: a state called 'thusness'. It is to us westerners unusual, but not entirely alien. Once perceived, it is found, in varying degrees, in all forms of art.

Have you never pinched the soft plastic stuff called potter's clay with wonder and delight, as many children do? Have you never walked the shallow water of a rocky beach like mine (at St Ives, Cornwall) and picked up the fine speckled sand between your toes, the detritus of granite and sea shells alive with tiny bits of quartz, feldspar, mica and iron stone? All lovely and irregular, full of enchantment. Such qualities are admired in Japan especially in connection with tea and Tea Ceremony wares.

Much influence has come to Japan, in the main from China and Korea, although it is seldom difficult to distinguish pots of these three countries from one another. Local characteristics are not so difficult to recognize even from various countrysides — Karatsu from Bizen, Onda from Seto. Local clay accounts for much character, also remoteness, such as at Onda, the period and source of influence as at Nai Shiro Gawa, where the villagers are direct descendants of the sixteenth-century Korean potters. Out of hundreds of potteries let me select Bizen and Tamba, probably the two oldest. At Bizen, the reddish, iron/rust coloured clay is very strong after long firing at high temperature, quite unglazed, except for wood ash falling and melting upon the exposed pots. The Tea Masters loved the austere simplicity of the old Iga and Bizen wares for their irregularity of form and natural effects due to great heat, even when

Bernard Leach at his pottery in St Ives, Cornwall

what we call distortion took place. This was often added to by cuts or pressures other than accidental, and, in later times, vulgarity and deliberation gained control, caused by a tug-of-war between intellect and intuition. Dr Yanagi and Shoji Hamada said that good creative craftsmen, with their wider outlook, if they are pure of heart, can stem the tides of decay better than the peasant craftsman.

In Bizen, clay or rotten stone erodes down the steep and barren mountain to the flat paddy-fields below. There, a good modern traditional potter, Toyo Kanashige, highly honoured by men of Tea and perception, bought his clay from a farmer when his field was fallow. He removed its crust of good soil, then the layer of plastic clay underneath, and carefully replaced the soil. Out of this raw material he picked out all the rougher impurities by hand, leaving in all that which would produce the fired-clay character in the final pots. Thus: a preservation of man's relationship with nature, handed down probably more than 2,000 years. We have to thank the recently deceased Toyo Kanashige, born in a background of country craftsmen, for facing the onrush of modernization with such insight and honesty. He may not have been a creative artist in the wider sense of travelled potters like Tomimoto or Hamada, but in his forms, apart from inherited or revived techniques, there was vitality and beauty which justified the recognition of his artistry.

At Tamba, that long, stern, narrow valley running due north and south, flanked with steep conical mountains, a river, a road and a few paddy-fields between, the potters carried their *shoyu* (soy sauce) and *sake* bottles over those mountain ranges to the old capital, Kyoto. The clay from the bottom of the slopes was never as good as at Bizen, nor as plastic, but from about the twelfth-century glazes began to be used. This must have been under distant Chinese influence, also recognizable in some of the shapes. In Bizen this is not so noticeable and both centres have their own strong but quite different Japanese character. Tamba has not produced what might rightly be called an artist-potter, although in the sixteenth century the famous Ninsei, Kenzan's master, was born there, but he was patronized by a tea-loving courtier of Kyoto. He travelled and eventually settled just outside the old capital. Bizen may be the oldest and most indigenous, but today Tamba still preserves the purest tradition of peasant pottery in Japan. Next I would place Onda and Koishibara in the central mountains of Kyushu in the south. There are many other potteries, vanishing or gone. This cannot be prevented, but a fragrance remains. Onda is dear to my heart — the remote mountain hamlet where I worked for two weeks amongst the most kind and unspoiled people. That unforgettable experience in the spring of 1935: the wild cherry flashed pink on the mountain side and Japanese nightingales sang in the bushes. Five hundred miles north to Tokyo, and afterwards, farewells at Tokyo Airport. As I walked across the tarmac an official ran to me with a letter. I opened the long scroll and there, upon the Japanese soft paper, were the imprints of the hands of the potters of Onda, of their wives, of their children . . . more moving than any spoken words.

Cinema *by Ken Wlaschin*

The Japanese cinema today might well be described as a cultural paradox. Although apparently widely known and recognized abroad, the great mass of Japanese films are virtually an unexplored territory as far as most western film critics and buffs are concerned. Only the tiniest percentage of Japanese films have ever been screened in Europe and America, yet Japanese films rank high in world critical polls of the best films ever made and directors like Akira Kurosawa, Yosijuro Ozu and Kenji Mizoguchi are securely lodged in the cinematic pantheon. While other major directors like Heinosuke Gosho remain virtually unknown despite the highest critical acclaim in Japan, *samurai* film star, Toshiro Mifune, has become probably the best-known Japanese individual in the world.

The Japanese cinema industry itself is possibly the only one in the world that bears real comparison with Hollywood in terms of organization, output and continuing quality. And it has suffered from the same financial decline brought on by the arrival of TV. Japan has been producing films for 75 years and has averaged over 400 films a year in peak times. But it wasn't until 1951, despite a few pre-war forays, that the West woke up to the fact that Japanese cinema existed. The revelation was *Rashomon* which stunned critics and audiences at the 1951 Venice Film Festival, winning the Grand Prix and opening up one of the major undiscovered artistic treasure troves in the world. Programmes as the National Film Theatre in London, the Cinemathèque Française in Paris and the Museum of Modern Art in New York revealed directors like Ozu and Mizoguchi who were not only among the masters of world cinema but also among the greatest artists ever produced by Japan. Indeed Ozu was often considered too purely Japanese to be truly appreciated by the West.

Today, the broad outlines of the Japanese cinematic art have become apparent though much is still unknown. Only a handful of Gosho's 90 films, for example, have been shown abroad and less than half of the works of both Ozu and Mizoguchi. Fuller

exploration and recognition will take many years. The whole area of Japanese 'popular entertainment' cinema is barely known. A recent series of films in London and Paris attempted to open up some of these areas. The highly popular *Woman Gambler* and *Blind Swordsmen* films were screened to fascinated audiences, films that in Japan have had commercial success comparable to the James Bond series. The Japanese 'ghost' film, the equivalent of the western horror film, is almost unknown and was represented by Nobuo Nakagawa's classic *Fantastic Tales of Yotsuya*. Unknown works by such modern masters of the cinema as Nagisa Oshima and Shohei Imamura caused as much excitement as the last film of veteran director Tomu Uchida. But series like these only begin to acquaint audiences with the wealth of Japanese cinema.

Commercial distribution of Japanese films in the West has been erratic and sporadic and even some of the masterpieces by the greatest directors have not yet received wide-spread showing. Akira Kurosawa, the director of *Rashomon* and *The Seven Samurai*, has had more commercial success abroad than any of his colleagues, but his last film, his first in colour and one of the best he has made, *Dodeska-Den*, has only been seen in Britain in the London Film Festival and the National Film Theatre. This amazing film (the title is onomatopoeic and represents the rattling sound of a streetcar) is the linked story of the inhabitants of a group of down-and-outers who live in a sordid congregation of shacks and rubbish on the edge of modern Tokyo. It is a deeply humane and poetic film, lively, funny and moving, and made with an extraordinary colour sense that perhaps could not have been attempted anywhere except in Japan.

Surprisingly, despite enormous borrowings from the West, the cinema in Japan has evolved into something uniquely Japanese. The ad-mixture of East and West can be seen in many ways, and is seen at its most striking and amusing in the interplay of cultural resonances in some of Kurosawa's works. His interest in the American thriller writer Dashiell Hammett, for example, led him to incorporate scenes from the novels *Red Harvest* and *The Glass Key* into a *samurai* film *Yojimbo* which won the Grand Prize at the Venice Film Festival. An Italian director, Sergio Leone, was so impressed by the film's similarities — not in relation to the American thriller — but to the Goldoni play *A Servant of Two Masters* that he modelled his own Western, *A Fistful of Dollars*, on it almost shot for shot. American filmmakers in their turn were so impressed with this Italian Western that they began to model their own work on the Italian example. And doubtless some American thriller-writer today is creating books under influences that have travelled around the world.

Kurosawa, however, is often accused of being the most 'western' of Japanese directors, the description really means only that he is not traditional in form and content. And tradition is important in the Japanese cinema in a way that is very alien to western film-goers. Japanese films are divided into rigid categories, almost as structured and tightly bound by conventions as the typical American Western. In other words, almost all Japanese films can be considered as genre films in which familiar patterns are worked out. Whereas the American Western continually returns to the stories of Billy the Kid or the gunfight at the OK Corral and re-tells them in a fresh way, usually reflecting popular feelings, the Japanese *samurai*-type film will return again and again to the stories of the loyal 47 Ronin or such sword-fighting heroes as Musashi Miyamoto.

Japanese films are divided into two large blocks — *jidai-geki* (period films) and *gendai-geki* (contemporary films). These blocks are further sub-divided into various kinds of *mono*, ie genres of film, concerned with self-sacrificing mothers or wives with problems or sportsmen or social criticism. Most Japanese filmmakers are aware that

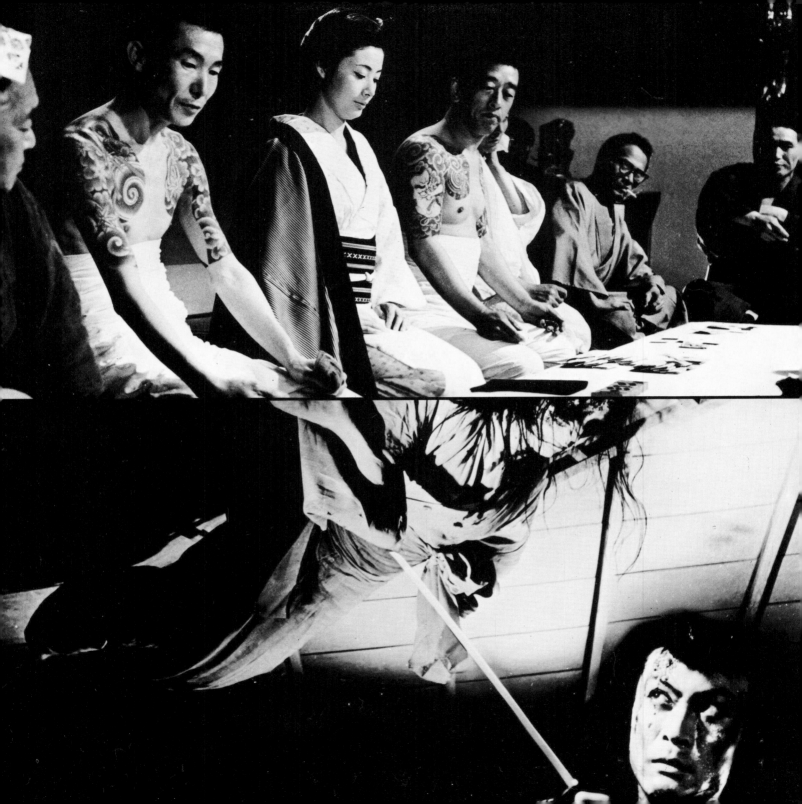

the film they are making is not a unique new creation but a continuation of past tradition that will be carried on in the future. Some few masters, like Kurosawa or Oshima, will break or mock the traditions within which they work; others, like Ozu, work apparently entirely inside the tradition, even re-making their own films, but filling them with a quiet beauty and profundity not unlike the later work of Rembrandt. If Kurosawa's films are often full of zest and movement and action, Ozu's films are alive with serenity and stillness and tranquillity. Both are very important artists but as different from each other as Wagner and Verdi.

It is sometimes said that Japanese films are 'slow' or have a slower tempo than American and European films. Perhaps it would be truer to say that the tempo of life and action in the traditional Japanese films runs at a different speed than in the West. But as accusations of 'slowness' have also been directed at such western filmmakers as Michelangelo Antonioni, it is apparent that the 'slowness' is in the viewer and not the film. New ways of looking and new attitudes about what to look for can be learned from even standard Japanese films. Indeed, there are puzzles and difficult aspects of Japanese cinema for the western viewer but these are primarily to do with cultural heritage and can be learned. Symbolic inserts and poetic images are used without explanation as audiences in Japan will already know what is represented. Traditional stories may have narrative incidents omitted if every Japanese viewer can be expected to know the story by heart. Puzzling influences from such earlier stage arts as *Nō* and *Kabuki* have been much exaggerated and indeed it is doubtful if deeper knowledge of these would be of real help to the western film critic.

What is sometimes puzzling, yet also delightful, is the deep concern that Japanese film people have about western attitudes to Japanese movies. Two of Japan's leading film personalities, Toshiro Mifune and Machiko Kyo, visited London and Paris in 1974 to help launch a new season of Japanese films. Their interest was cultural, not commercial, far away in spirit from a Hollywood star drum-beating for his latest film. Mr Mifune, star of many of Kurosawa's best films, felt that interest in Europe could even help boost the flagging industry in Japan. Although he is now working primarily in television (he has his own studio and at one time made three 52-episode series simultaneously) and is the most honoured of actors, he still felt the Japanese cinema had many things to learn from Europe. Miss Kyo, the very beautiful and modest star of such films as *Rashomon* and *Ugetsu Monogatari*, is also primarily working in TV today but was highly hopeful that the era of sex and violence in the Japanese cinema was ending. Her personal preferences in films were towards the 'romantic and the mysterious' but her summing up of the best of Japanese cinema was remarkably appropriate: 'One is always trying to make something beautiful and lasting but you do not realise until years later the success you have had'.

The ideographic world

by Fosco Maraini

The Far East may be many things — Mount Fuji and the Great Wall of China, the gardens of Kyoto, shopping in Hong Kong, the palaces of Peking, priceless jade, a *geisha* smiling, the splendour of pearls — but it is also an ocean of mysterious signs, an ideographic empire. As one lands in the far East, anywhere, one is immediately struck by the presence of hieroglyphs: on walls, roofs, shops, in books, newspapers, accompanying films, on the backs of vehicles — everywhere. Initially one feels thwarted (I have studied for nearly twenty years, I have a university degree, yet here I am, illiterate!), but one is soon enticed by the fascination of it all (What does that exquisite little knot of lines mean? Happy love? Ultimate truth? Or simply cabbage, slippers, a bicycle). It does not really matter. Meanings seem irrelevant in that precise and subtly balanced dance of lines, dots, squares, bold downward strokes, tapering tails, flying commas. After the first humiliation one is exalted by the presence of so much, and such rich abstract beauty.

Innumerable questions rush to mind. Can this cryptic flow of arabesques really be used to convey meaning? Granted, it may have its uses in poetry and on memorial stones, but what about laundry bills, political leader articles, machine handling instructions, handbooks of engineering or economics? How is it that countries so highly developed and so progressive still use this archaic and cumbersome system of writing?

Let us take a close look at the ideographic script and see how it works: it may turn out to be less archaic and cumbersome than it appears. Take, for example, the universal sign for a *dangerous bend*, seen along most of our roads. Imagine you are travelling by car at 60 or 70 miles an hour. Suddenly the sign catches your eye; in a hundredth of a second you grasp its significance, your foot applies the pressure to the brakes and you negotiate the bend perfectly. But had the same information been conveyed through phonetic writing, and the expression 'Dangerous Bend' been spelled out in full, there probably would have been no time to read the sign — and you might have been involved in an accident.

With the ideographic system of writing, information leaps immediately from the eye to the mind, bypassing the ear. And this is not because each sign is a 'picture' (there are only a few dozen simplified images among the 2,000-odd Japanese characters in normal use) but rather because each ideogram acts as a highly individualized symbol. With a phonetic script, words must be first coded into signs which stand for sounds, then decoded from signs to sounds, and finally from sounds to meanings — a complicated and roundabout route.

An ideographic system of writing is evidently harder to learn, but once it has been mastered, the author's ideas, thoughts, emotions, are conveyed with far greater impact to his reader. Scanning a page of ideographic script is like taking a walk at high speed through the traffic signals of the mind: meanings flash, jump directly from page to eye with extraordinary vividness. The Japanese rightly say that their own language when written phonetically appears 'out of focus' *(pinto ga awanai)*. The ideographic script hugs life much more closely, resulting in faster perception.

So, as the need for speed in transmitting information assumes growing importance, the West is discovering the value of the ideogram — though few people may be aware of such a fact. Look at the ever-growing tribe of traffic signals: a small pump for a petrol station; a bed for a motel; knife and fork for a restaurant; two children for a school; a cow, where cattle may be crossing the road. For communicative speed the cumbersome phonetic coding and decoding of sounds cannot match the simple, explosive ideogram.

Comparing the two systems of writing shows that the alphabet is not as superior as one tends to think. For all practical purposes, the ideographic system is as good as our own. Alphabets have been known to the people of the Far East since the introduction of Buddhism, and Sanskrit texts appreciated nearly two thousand years ago. Thus, if they continue using the ideographic script it is not only for reasons of tradition and aesthetics, but for practicality.

Ideograms were first invented in the Far East by the Chinese during, or possibly before, the Shang dynasty (1766-1122 BC). For some two thousand years the signs slowly developed, undergoing many transformations through an internal evolution of the system and by substantial changes in technique. Initially, ideograms were engraved on hard surfaces (bone, metal, stone), but gradually, with man's discovery of the brush, ink and paper, a revolution took place: most lines became straight, circles and ovals were turned into squares and rectangles. By the end of the second century AD (the later Han dynasty) ideograms were generally standardized; and there have been few changes since then.

Chinese cultural superiority made it practically mandatory for neighbouring peoples to adopt the ideographic script and emerge from barbarism into the light of civilization. The Japanese took their ideograms from the Koreans at some time in the sixth century AD, and quite naturally called them *han-signs (Kan-ji)* — *Han* being both the name of a major dynasty and of China itself.

Eventually the whole of the Far East became a vast ideographic pool. Books written in one region could be read and understood anywhere from Central Asia to Japan, from Vietnam to Manchuria or Korea. This is easily explained: while alphabets divide, ideograms unite. An alphabet reproduces the actual sounds of a language and isolates, consolidates the words of a single nation or tribe; an ideogram carries meanings which, though not always universal, are at least far more international. The word 'man' is not the same as 'homme', 'andras' or 'Mensch', but a rose is a rose is a rose at all latitudes and longitudes. Our numbers and mathematical symbols function in a way similar to ideograms. For instance, the number 88 is written uniformly all over Europe but pronounced in twenty or thirty different linguistic forms.

With time, ideograms multiplied inordinately. One great dictionary published in 1716, during the reign of Emperor K'ang Hsi, contains about 40,000 signs. It is true, as Leon Wieger says, that 34,000 of them are 'monstrosities of no practical use', but even the remaining five or six thousand are undoubtedly a heavy burden on the mind. In ages of aristocratic leisure this may have been an interesting challenge to scholarship, but in our more recent, practical times the problems of mass education have demanded a drastic reduction. In 1946 the Japanese Government published a list of 1,850 essential ideograms *(Toyo kanji)*, many of them in simplified form, which are now the only ones taught in the schools and normally used by the Press.

When the Communists came to power in China they did very much the same thing, but their choice and their simplification have been different. If, one way or another, the Chinese and Japanese had been able to work together on the details of this operation, a cultural watershed of immense significance and importance could have been defined with some rationality. As it is, the agelong unity of the Far East has now been shattered. Modern Chinese and Japanese peoples can only barely, vaguely understand each other's writings, unless they have made a special study of each other's language. The name of Mao Tse-tung, for instance, is written in three noticeably different ways in China, Japan and Hong Kong/Formosa. Worthy of note, too, is the fact that the Vietnamese have adopted the Roman alphabet, while the Koreans insist on using their native *hangul* script. So, confusion and fragmentation have replaced the unity of ages.

Apart from graphic differences in the actual delineation of *kanji*, a Japanese text can easily be distinguished from a Chinese one by the presence of *kana* signs. What are they? For the Japanese it was not enough to adopt the Chinese script; they had to adapt it to a language of an entirely different structure. Chinese is monosyllabic, Japanese polysyllabic; Chinese has no inflections, Japanese in many cases acts as an inflected language. Certain signs were soon invented — tradition says by the sage Kobo Daishi (774-835) — to set down in a simple way the many suffixes and particles of the Japanese language, the inflections of its verbs and adjectives. These were the *kana* (temporary, informal, unauthorized) letters. Two scripts of this type emerged: one more rigid and formal, the *kata-kana* (hard *kana*), the other more cursive and informal, the *hira-gana* (ordinary, simple, humble *kana*). Nowadays *kata-kana* is extensively used for the innumerable foreign loanwords which have drifted into the Japanese language, such as *surriru* (thrill), *Markusu* (Marx), *arbaito* (side-job, from the German Arbeit) — to mention but a few.

Most systems of writing have an origin in common with painting. In the Far East writing and painting have remained intimately united to this day. This is easily understandable, considering that the basic technical instrument — a brush — is used in both forms of art. It is also clear that a common tool produces lines which are similar, if not identical. Oriental aesthetics have developed this art to a refined nicety. Chiang-yee reminds us that 'the good painter is he who can play the line-game well'. The strokes of painters are divided into many classes, such as 'iron-wire', 'willow leaf', 'bamboo-leaf', 'silk-thread', 'bending-weed', 'earth-worm', 'water-wrinkle' and so on. Calligraphers make their strokes with the same fastidious scrutiny and attention.

Can the extraordinary Japanese sensitivity to lines be somehow related to the ideographic air breathed since childhood? That elegant and subtle network of lines which is a Japanese home (*tatami* mats and their geometry, sliding *shoji* doors and windows with their chess-board of paper and wood, beams and rafters in the ceiling) responds to the same balances and rhythms which regulate characters such as *kaku* (to write) or *koto* (thing), with their serrated horizontal strokes firmly bound by a bold vertical shaft. Straight lines meet diagonal ones in freer counterpoints, both in the ideographic space, such as in *mairu* (to go) or *ware* (I), and all through country life, from tiles on a roof to seedlings in a rice field.

A very distinctive linear motif, appearing in many ideograms, could jokingly be called 'the pagodic': a dainty little umbrella crowning a castle of lines. The 'pagodic' passes naturally and gracefully from ideograms to roofs, to hats, to tombstones, to lanterns, to floats in a festival procession — finally merging into the primeval outline of hills and volcanoes.

Many such families of lines can be followed all through the texture of Japanese life, art, writing, nature. There is a square world, there are flowing and flying worlds, there are worlds of masculine power and subtle feminine worlds too. The *hiragana* alphabet, and practically all characters written in the cursive *(sosho)* form, lead us into the land of circles and tangles — where we also meet gorgeous rotating symbols (the *mitsu-tomoye*) together with umbrellas, lacquered wheels, bolts, ash-trays and fishermen's nets holding their shiny glass floats, like mysterious jewels out of the depths.

Plates 22-25 inclusive: *Expressions of Japan's ideographic world.*

Plate 26: *A study in shapes. Stall in a temple precinct.*

122

Kanji for *three* or *pilgrimage*

川

Kanji for *river*

Hiragana script: inflection 'o'

茶

Kanji for *tea*

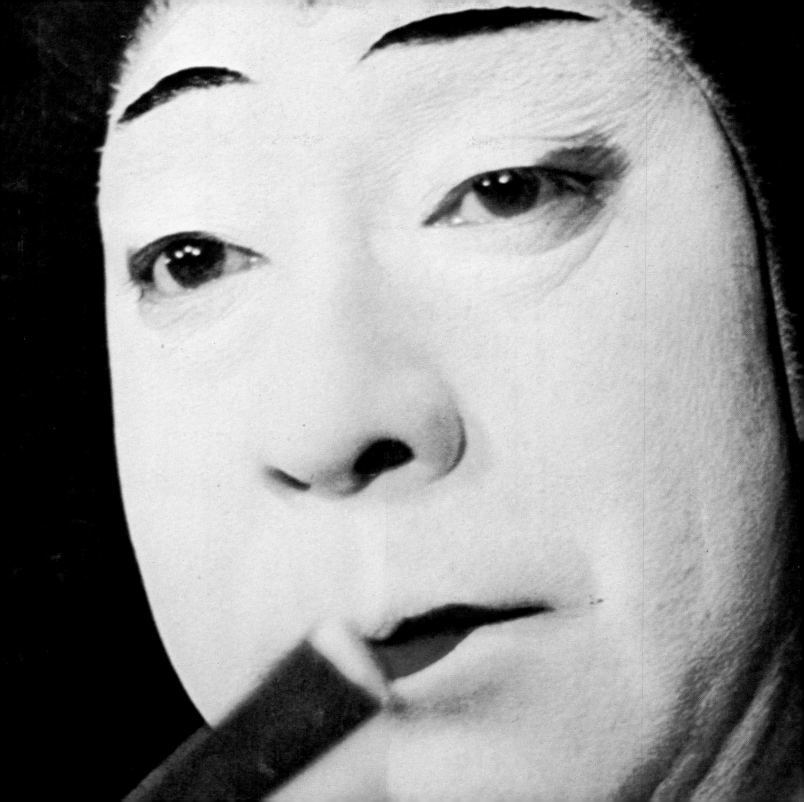

Japan in concert *by Bernard Keeffe*

Since the late 1960s it has been difficult to write about Japan without overworking the clichés of astonishment. We have bored ourselves silly with superlatives. But we delude ourselves if we regard this astonishing people as a nation of industrious automatons, and I think their achievements in music should help to correct this view. The trouble is, we know so little about them. Some years ago I visited the United States to make a TV programme for the BBC about what I glibly called 'the largest music school in the world'. It had twelve hundred students. Later I visited the Kunitachi school in Tokyo. It had seven thousand students.

In 1853, when Commodore Matthew C. Perry landed near Yokohama, bringing the historic letter from the President of the United States that was to open Japan to the West, he was accompanied by the band of the US Marines playing *Hail Columbia*. The Japanese, drawn up along the beach in endless ranks of mediaeval splendour, were astonished at the sight and sound of clarinets, cornets and euphoniums, and talked for weeks of the 'strange music of the West'. But now, just over a hundred years later, their descendants show a mastery of western musical techniques quite beyond the imagination of Perry and his bandmaster, and have made music one of the most significant aspects of their daily life.

One of the earliest promoters of western music in Japan was an American music teacher — John Luther Mason. He introduced class singing into Japanese schools and made the great traditional songs of the West as familiar in Kobe as in Cleveland. You can still hear Japanese children singing a lively version of *Sur le pont d'Avignon*, and the tune (but not the words) of *Auld lang Syne* is bawled out with as much fervour in the Ginza as in the pubs of Glasgow. For years this was the limit of Japanese musical culture, but gradually people began to learn instruments, English and French bandmasters were imported and even orchestras were formed. The most successful of these was undoubtedly the New Symphony Orchestra, formed under the direction of the Viscount Hidemaro Konoye, in the early 'twenties. He was a conductor skilled enough to give concerts and make records with the Berlin Philharmonic, and rich enough to maintain his own orchestra in Tokyo. But the basic problem was still unsolved: symphonies and sonatas never ceased to be foreign music. They were performed with care, but sounded as awkward as those inevitable morning suits that sat so uneasily on Japanese shoulders. What then has happened in the last thirty years, that Japan should have become one of the most important countries of the musical world?

I think the answer is that after the war the Japanese accepted western habits and western music in a way that their traditions had never before allowed. The 'strange music of the West' simply stopped being strange and foreign, and therefore suspect. It was accepted as just music. It offered a release for emotions at a time of considerable stress, and the Japanese learned to get the same sort of uplift from the symphonies of Beethoven and Brahms as any audience in Europe or America. The concerts were given chiefly by the orchestra of the NHK (the equivalent of the BBC) under visiting conductors from America and Europe. It was not easy to cope with post-war poverty, and the violinists often had to tie the strings together when they broke. But the orchestra played with fervour to large and enraptured audiences. The coming of the LP record rapidly helped to train their musical sensibilities, and made western music a

Plates 27 and 28: Bunraku *puppet face and* Kabuki *actor.*

Plate 29: *Archery contest in the grounds of the Meiji Shrine, Tokyo.*

Plate 30: *Cormorant fishing on the Uji River.*

familiar everyday experience. Since then the development has been astonishing — there are now some six symphony orchestras in Tokyo alone, playing to packed audiences in a magnificent concert hall.

The conductor Leopold Stokowski prophesies that world orchestras of the future will be filled with Japanese violinists. In making such a claim he is underlining the desperate problem that faces so many orchestras today: the growing shortage of good string players. Fewer and fewer young people are prepared to undertake the long and difficult hours of practice, only to spend their careers in the boring obscurity of the back-desks of an orchestra. Imagine then the fascinated delight of conductors, managers and agents when they saw a film of three thousand Japanese children playing the violin with unbelievable unanimity and assurance. Surely Japan has produced nothing in music so overwhelming as the teaching method evolved by Shinichi Suzuki.

The Suzuki school of Talent Education is to be found, not in Tokyo or any other city of the great urban sprawl that stretches along the Inland Sea, but in the small town of Matsumoto, the gateway to the Japan Alps. It is a measure of this remarkable man's achievement that thirty years ago he set up his school in an area where, not only was there virtually no musical education, but few of the inhabitants actually recognized a violin when they saw it. Today, the products of that school are to be found in orchestras all over the world from Boston to Berlin. Shinichi Suzuki is an amazing combination of musician, teacher, philosopher and psychologist. He believes that a child should learn music just as he learns his native language — by hearing his mother speak it. The first stage does in fact involve the mother, who must herself learn to play on a violin the simple tunes which form the basis of the method. The children, from the age of eighteen months, are encouraged to listen and then copy the mother's playing, always by ear and imitation, without the problem of reading until much later, just as with the spoken language. The results of this attitude and the efficacy of his method are undeniable. At the age of three or four, children can play with a perfect arm and wrist position (a rare achievement at any age in the West), well in tune, and with lively and accurate rhythm. What is more, these happy children love to play — in fact they have to be restrained from practising too much.

Suzuki's sense of dedication reflects the traditional place of honour that a teacher is given in Japan. To be called *sensei* (teacher) was and is a token of deep respect and love, which has no counterpart in the West. I found the same depth of purpose and respect for his students in Hideo Saito, the outstanding figure in the Toho Gakuen, probably the finest private music school in Tokyo. (It also happens to be quite small — having only three thousand students!) Saito was trained as a 'cellist in Germany and played in Viscount Konoye's orchestra. Later on in his career he took up conducting, and now is regarded as one of the world's finest teachers of that elusive art. He numbers pupils from America and Canada amongst his students. But his star pupil is undoubtedly Seiji Ozawa, whose work with the Toronto, San Francisco and Chicago orchestras has put him amongst the world's most admired conductors.

The dedication of the *sensei* is echoed, I think, in the paternalistic attitude of many industrial and commercial tycoons. Paternalism suits the Japan of today, and if nothing else the daily hymn to the virtues of productivity presupposes a company choir. Such choirs form the basis of a flourishing choral movement, and each Christmas Japan, like England and America, comes out in a rash of Messiahs — except that Beethoven's 9th symphony runs a close second in Tokyo.

This paternalism, not unmixed with a shrewd business sense, has thrown up another unique organization: the Yamaha Music Foundation. This trust was set up with money provided by the great Yamaha firm, which makes everything from motorcycles to marimbas. The Yamaha Foundation provides facilities and teachers for the young and the amateur to learn a musical instrument, either at home or in its lavishly equipped music camp at Nemu-no-Sato.

But what of composition? No nation can claim a healthy musical culture if it boasts only technical or interpretive success. Here Japan is in a dilemma. There is no question that creative genius flourishes in the traditional soil. Every German composer, for example, knows that he is part of a line that stretches back to Bach; the Italian musician in Venice works in a setting where great music flourished three hundred years ago; in England Benjamin Britten and Michael Tippett hand on a tradition that derived from Purcell. How can Japanese composers take up the apparatus of western music without the foundation on which it was built? For a while they tried to copy standard European models, and produced some feeble plastic blooms. Later, they succumbed to a spurious international modernism that has enfeebled music even in those countries which can claim a strong national tradition. It is the kind of music that wins votes at international festivals, but empties halls in the home town. However, it is exciting to see a new generation of Japanese composers finding a more inspired solution to their dilemma. Toshiro Mayuzumi, for example, is an inescapable figure. He has been a conductor, TV commentator, a composer of highly successful film scores for Hollywood, and is the author of the pre-announcement jingle for the bullet-train. Here is a man who might be expected to challenge Bernstein as an international whizz-kid of music. But he has chosen to turn to the traditional sounds of Japan, and in his *Bungaku*, for instance, has re-created the idiom of ancient music in terms of the modern symphony orchestra. He believes that Japan can make her greatest contribution to international music by being proudly Japanese. Certainly, this view is borne out by our own experience. We admire Italian opera, Russian ballet, German symphonies, American jazz; each nation offers its own contribution to the world's treasure-house of music, and like man himself, offers most when most honestly itself.

Perhaps the best composer in this new Japanese idiom is Toru Takemitsu. Not only has he used the modern orchestra, like Mayuzumi, but he has combined it with the traditional instruments of Japan — the *shakuhachi*, a kind of recorder, and the *koto*, a sort of horizontal harp — in his most successful post-war composition, *November Steps*. This approach has been taken even further by a group called the Nipponia Ensemble. It is in effect a small orchestra of ancient instruments played with some of the freedom and virtuosity of their modern counterparts, in works specially written by such composers as Minoru Miki. The results are fascinating: new sounds, new textures, new harmonies, new melodic shapes — a strange and delightful world — especially for ears battered by the acerbities of our avant-garde music.

Music in Japan stands at a crucial and yet ironic state of development. At a time when musicians and audiences in the West grow more pessimistic about the prospects for opera, the symphony orchestra, and for the whole elaborate machinery of nineteenth-century music, Japan is excitedly revelling in this her new discovery. We have taught her a lot, and the last few years have shown how the pupil has begun to catch up with the master. Perhaps we can now in our turn learn something — about education, about composition, even about our own traditions seen through the penetrating gaze of a Mayuzumi. Perhaps it is our turn to learn something now, from the strange new music of the East.

Ukiyo-e: the real world of make-believe
by David G. Chibbett

Ukiyo-e is a term with which anyone at all interested in Japan will be familiar. Its literal meaning is 'pictures of the floating world' (*ukiyo* being originally a Buddhist epithet symbolising the transience of life), and it used to describe the paintings, prints and book illustrations of Japan's greatest period of popular art, spanning from the end of the seventeenth century to the Meiji Restoration in 1868 and shortly thereafter. To many people indeed, the art of Japan is *ukiyo-e*, and the rapidly increasing prices fetched in the auction rooms of the world by *ukiyo-e* works are indicative that they are bigger business than ever before.

A great deal has been written by Japanese and western authorities on *ukiyo-e* as *art*, but far less has been written about the society which produced it. Of course, the world so brilliantly portrayed by such artists as Utamaro, Harunobu, Hokusai and Hiroshige no longer exists, and it may be that very fact which gives it such a powerful appeal today. It is questionable whether people who spend vast sums on the works of these great artists fully realise that what they are purchasing are in some senses no more than the mass-produced product of one of the world's first true consumer societies. The social background of *ukiyo-e* is consequently well worth investigating.

When the Tokugawa family seized power in the early years of the seventeenth century, one of the most urgent problems facing them was to find a system which would ensure peace for Japan after more than two hundred years of intermittent civil war. One of the methods chosen to achieve this was the enforcement of a rigid social structure under which society was divided into four basic categories; at the top of the social system came the *samurai*, the professional warrior class; then came the peasant on whose labours the wealth of the country (rice) rested; next was the artisan who, although not as important as the peasant, could at least show some finished product for his work; finally, at the bottom of society, were the merchants and tradesmen who bought and sold without any evident end product. That this and the other methods employed were successful in fulfilling their purpose is shown by the fact that Japan enjoyed a period of more than two hundred and fifty years of comparative peace until they were suddenly confronted by the West in the mid-nineteenth century. There were, however, some interesting and unforeseen social side-effects.

Ultimately, peace and security meant that the *samurai*, often men of considerable talents, became redundant in their original capacity and were forced to seek some new outlet for their abilities. At the same time, the tradesmen class built up considerable surplus wealth, but, denied any active rôle in government, they had only limited opportunities for disposing of it in a creative way. Frequently, particularly in the major cities (Edo, Osaka, Kyoto and to a lesser extent Nagoya), the men of these socially estranged classes came together with common interests. The centre of their joint activities was usually the city pleasure quarters (the most notable of these being the Yoshiwara in Edo) which largely grew up in response to their needs.

Pleasure quarters need not be taken as implying only brothels (although these, of course, were an important ingredient), because their object was to cover and provide entertainment in every form, from music to poetry, and from wrestling to the theatre. As time went by, the term *ukiyo* came to be used not as a symbol for the transience of life, but for the *pleasures* of that transient life. These very pleasures surrounded the residents of the Yoshiwara district (and its imitators in other cities) and therefore it is not surprising that when the artists who lived there searched for suitable material, they turned to what they knew best — the life and society of the Yoshiwara.

In many senses the Yoshiwara residents stimulated the demand for such pictures. The *Kabuki* drama, for example, was so popular that the people who frequented it were keen to possess portraits of their favourite actors. Courtesans fell into a similar category — everyone wanted their pictures (and here it should be remembered that courtesans were not simply prostitutes, but usually accomplished musicians and poets into the bargain). In the days before the invention of photography and when it was still far too expensive for the majority to commission painted portraits, wood block prints, cheaply produced in great numbers, were the ideal solution to the problem. This, of course, is why so very many prints are of actors and courtesans, and the landscape print which developed later again reflects the desire of the people to have pictures of the places they lived in or saw frequently. Thus the art of *ukiyo-e* was born — to satisfy a demand for cheaply produced pictures of everyday life for people who were often illiterate or semi-illiterate. This, however, is only one side to the question.

It has frequently been stated that the art of *ukiyo-e* is realistic, in other words that it accurately and minutely portrays the real life of real people. This is a false concept which belies the true nature of the society which produced it. The idea of people devoted to a life of pleasure is these days an appealing one (although when J. E. De Becker published his history of the Yoshiwara., *The Nightless City*, in 1899 he was censured for appearing to sanction immorality), and there is great appeal, too, in the idea of *ukiyo-e* as 'classless art', which indeed it was, for woodblock prints would be found on the walls of a *samurai* house and peasant cottage alike.

It is true also that a great deal of what we know about Japanese society in the Edo period derives from *ukiyo-e* prints and illustrations. In this sense the appellation 'realistic' is deserved. However, *ukiyo-e* art is only realistic in the sense that the *Tale of Genji* is realistic. For example, a reader of the *Tale of Genji* could easily carry away with him the idea that life in 11th-century Japan was one long round of poetry contests, moon viewing and secret amorous liaisons. Certainly, it may have been like that for some, but for the vast majority of the population 'reality' lay in unceasing labour in the fields, often with little to eat. In the same way, we are apt to look at prints of beautiful courtesans boating on the river, or of splendid landscapes and think that this is how life really was.

Fundamentally, the world of Genji and the world of the Yoshiwara were escapist, which is an odd common feature to find in view of the fact that the two societies and cultures were six centuries apart and stemming from completely different social backgrounds. Basically, the Yoshiwara, like the aristocrat court of eleventh-century Kyoto, was a sub-world far removed from reality. There is little evidence, for example, in the writings of the *ukiyo-e* artists, *kyoka* poets and others who lived in the Yoshiwara to indicate that they were aware of the fact that within the very same city people were dying of hunger every day. It seems unlikely that they did not know this, and so the only conclusion one can draw is that they did not care. Of course, to criticise them for this as unreasonable as criticising their art for what it did *not* portray rather than for what it did portray. This situation, however, does serve to demonstrate the fact that the Yoshiwara was an isolated community which for all its cultural brilliance had effectively cut itself off from the outside world. It was a kind of exclusive club, the membership qualifications for which were artistic or literary ability, or at least the ability to appreciate these qualities in others.

In essence, one might say that the art of *ukiyo-e* was yet another manifestation of the Japanese facility for separating the production of art and literature from reality (the history of the arts in Japan is filled with similar examples of small groups cutting themselves off from the outside world and communicating basically with only each other), but viewed from this distance it seems to matter very little. Lack of realism as the underlying concept of apparently 'realistic' art is a small price to pay for the enjoyment which the glories of *ukiyo-e* art have given in the past and continue to give to Japanese and westerner alike.

Japan's living theatre

by Charles J. Dunn

Theatre audiences in Japan are as varied as the theatres themselves, and that is saying a great deal for, as with almost all art forms, Japan has abandoned hardly anything that used to flourish in the past. If you seek hard and long enough you will find all the old art forms still being carried on somewhere.

I was astonished some years ago to find an old-style touring *Kabuki* troupe performing in a village theatre — associated, as is nearly always the case in the country, with the local *shinto* shrine. The audience was I suppose predictable. It was in the autumn, and the crops had been harvested. The theatre consisted of nothing but a stage; there was no accommodation for the audience. In earlier times spectators just sat around on the ground in the open air. Nowadays, there isn't much difference except that we were all clustered under a marquee which, I must confess, did little to keep out the cold evening air of the hills behind Kobe. Everybody was dressed quite informally and most people fought off the cold with the help of a bottle or two, and a helping of *oden* (a form of country stew) — unkindly described by one foreigner as 'a lot of boiled-up old roots' but delicious to all the connoisseurs who had purchased some from the stalls at the back of the tent.

Such was the composition of the audience, an audience, in fact, which differs little from its big-city counterpart at Osaka. Indeed, at a later visit to Osaka's New Kabuki Theatre, for example, I noticed that the audience was largely a local one with rather

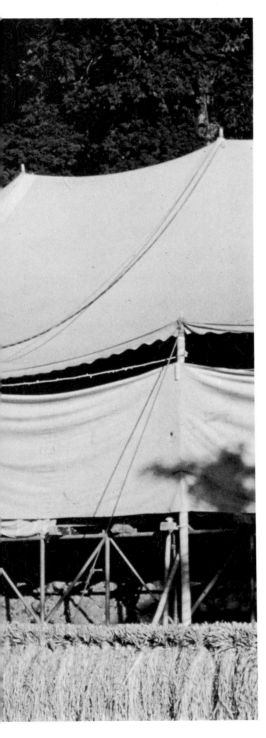

more old ladies than old men (there were very few young people), and on this occasion it was clear that everybody present was there to see the play. To see the play? Is there any other reason why one goes to the theatre, you might ask? In Japan — in the big Tokyo *Kabuki* theatres — there could well be other reasons. On more than one occasion in Tokyo I have thought of profiting from an unexpectedly free half day by taking in a *Kabuki* programme, only to find on arriving at the theatre that the ordinary public were not being allowed in, it having been taken over for the day by some large business firm for a company outing.

Kabuki has been more spectacle than drama ever since that day, some 370 years ago, when O-Kuni, the alleged priestess from the great shrine at Izumo, came to Kyoto to put on her show at the Kitano shrine. The fact that this was a Buddhist performance, characterised by singing a religious text and dancing to the ringing of a gong which she also carried, need surprise nobody, even though she was ostensibly raising a contribution for a *shinto* shrine.

There has been little intolerance in Japanese religious life, especially as between Buddhism and Shintoism and in any case O-Kuni soon paired up with her boy-friend to put on much more secular attractions.

But, to return to the present day, the Tokyo *Kabuki* Theatre has several restaurants and snack counters, not to mention souvenir shops, and even a large colour television set outside the auditorium. Exhibitions are also held there occasionally so that there is plenty to look at and spend one's money on without watching a play at all. And even while you are watching a play there is nothing to stop you having a snack, or even reading the paper, since the house lights are often left on except when the scene takes place at Night, or it is a new play in which conventions of the western theatre seem to apply.

Not surprisingly, of course, Japanese theatre construction and stage technology are very advanced. Japanese audiences have always been willing to pay to see startling effects; whereas the more aesthetically inclined who indulge in *Nō* plays have preferred the less extravagant staging that their more refined art demands even though *Nō* costumes are invariably quite spectacular.

Special effects involve the use of traps, lifts and revolving stages, all of which the Japanese seem to have invented quite independently of similar developments in the West.

The National Theatre in Tokyo brings in performers for each season to put on *Kabuki* and other plays on its large stage; it also stages the puppet theatre (*Bunraku*) as well as all sorts of music and dance performances on the smaller stage. In short, the National Theatre's staging capabilities are immense; not unnaturally, it enjoys indulging in spectacular effects such as a real waterfall on the stage with a pool below it containing enough water to allow the characters to plunge in and enjoy a prolonged, watery sword-fight. The National Theatre also sees itself as a museum of drama. For example, it can afford to put on plays that have not been seen for a very long time — directed by the most distinguished scholars in a particular field. Indeed, one of the reasons for going to the National Theatre is to see unfamiliar plays, not well-known pieces in which the emotional stimulus and response is predictable.

Meanwhile, *Nō* theatre-goers are changing a little too. Once the audience was virtually confined to addicts whose one object in life was to learn to sing the rôles or play the instruments in the plays they were attending. And so they followed the performance earnestly with book in hand, but paid little attention to the *Kyogen* comic interludes. One thing that is happening today, however, is that younger people are finding the comic interludes of great interest, not so much for their excellent acting and inspired clowning, but rather as examples of earthy, peasant literature, a sort of

141

comic drama of protest which did not hesitate to make fun of gods, warriors and priests — all very different from the solemn ritualistic *Nō* on the one hand and the merchant values of the *Kabuki* on the other.

Japan's other traditional drama, in which she leads the world, is the highly developed doll theatre. Here again the old rural audience still survives, notably on the island of Awaji, Tokushima in Shikoku, the island of Sado off Niigata and in the Chichibu mountains behind Tokyo. Particularly energetic performers survive in Hachioji, just west of Tokyo, where one operator (instead of the three that share the work in the *Bunraku* of Osaka and elsewhere), with a roller strapped to his bottom works a puppet by himself. Even more exhausting is what goes on in Kitabaru, in Kyushu, where one man darts around the stage in a crouched position, like a Cossack dancer, with the puppets attached to his feet and hands. These country groups perform at festive times, and are still assured of their audiences.

As for the central *Bunraku* group, based in Osaka, but giving regular performances in the small hall of the National Theatre, I have the impression that it would probably now be faced with financial problems were it not given various subsidies. The traditional audiences of Osaka are dying out from sheer old age but a younger audience is returning, aware that here Japan has something that is unique in the world, and something that should be encouraged.

The audiences I have mentioned are often motivated by other things than a simple search for entertainment. This is even more true of those that go to *shingeki*, the 'new theatre'. This is the theatre of what might be called the orthodox radical intellectual. The repertory is composed partly of translated material and partly of modern Japanese plays. The companies presenting these performances are organized on a form of co-operative basis; the stars don't receive large salaries but there is a strong group spirit, typically Japanese. The actors supplement their incomes with film and television work.

In view of the earnest spirit of this 'new theatre' it is not surprising that the audiences, too, tend to be serious. They very rarely go to be entertained but rather to learn, to find out about foreign drama, or to nourish their social conscience. It follows that they are very attentive, rather solemn, and rather sparing in their response. In fact it is typical of Japanese audiences over the whole range of drama that they are much less effusive in their applause than in the West. And in *Kabuki* there are no curtain calls, just a few seconds of clapping and away everyone goes.

Kabuki, it is true, has a special sort of audience reaction which consists of shouting, at appropriate moments, such things as the equivalent of 'We've been waiting for you', or the names of favourite actors as they appear, with remarks suggesting that they are due for promotion or the like.

It is also worth remembering, incidentally, that many department stores have theatres; there are also one or two magnificent houses such as the Imperial Theatre, and the theatre within the Japanese Life Insurance Headquarters Building, which provide opera or the modern western-style musicals. This kind of theatrical entertainment is very popular, as indeed are the girlie shows in Asakusa in Tokyo, and the spectacular all-female Takarazuka revues.

The pragmatic builders

by Fosco Maraini

Many travellers to Japan are struck by the confusion and lack of sensitivity in design and layout of Japanese cities. Sir Sacheverell Sitwell (born 1897), though reacting very positively to the people in Tokyo, was distressed by the city's appearance. No metropolis of comparative size, he notes, 'has less to show in the sphere of architecture and of art. There is indeed no building worth mentioning' (*Bridge of the Brocade Sash*, 1959). Since then Kenzo Tange's Olympic sports centre has gone up (1964) and some other fine specimens of modern architecture have appeared here and there, and there are some new bright stars glimmering on the horizon; but the original haphazard, sprawling forest has changed very little.

A confirmed optimist, of course, will invariably locate something he believes to be beautiful — and rightly so — even in Tokyo's muddle of shacks, yards, nondescript concrete boxes and huge steel-framed colossi. This beautiful 'something' could be the time just after sun-set, for instance. At that miraculous moment, says James Kirkup, there are 'towers and sheets and gloves and rivers of neon in stunning profusion, a wild razzle-dazzle of colours and shapes and movements, fierce and delicate, restrained and violent against the afterglow of sunset' (*These Horned Islands*, 1962).

To this I would add another more dynamic dimension of beauty, one quintessentially modern, one you 'discover' as you drive along the elevated motorway encircling the very heart of Tokyo. Most highways are straight and unimaginative. Not this one! Irregular turns follow one another with sudden dips and climbs. Driving, here, is diving. One is led, as in a dance, by the ribbon of asphalt which plunges through sudden tunnels, soars above mazes of bridges or crashes through a forest of towers, while down below, Tokyo's great avenues, choked with the metal flow of cars, rotate madly like vineyards seen from a speeding train.

But, in the final analysis, we all have to face the facts: the magic of neon and sunset, the wonder of a capricious drive through twentieth century megapolitan space, fade away. What remains is a lot of grey cement, unidentifiable objects with turrets and spires, or a giant thirty storeys high crushing a diminutive fossil Shinto shrine — while wires, a cobweb of wires, shred space to smithereens above our heads. The same

143

question returns again and again: why the lack of poetry, why such unredeemed ugliness in a land of such natural splendour, in a country inhabited by notorious lovers of beauty?

If Tokyo alone were an exception, the confusion and congestion could be justified, perhaps, on the grounds of the urgency of rebuilding following the mass destruction of the city in the great earthquake of 1923 and the bombing of 1945. But Tokyo is no exception. Not even Kyoto, for example, is so different these days. Up until a few decades ago Kyoto, with its row upon row of wooden houses and typical roofs of grey-black tiles, was a city of great charm. Now everything is changing at great speed: nondescript buildings of alarming proportions are replacing the old, historical houses, which are actually condemned to extinction by law, because — it is said — they are too great a fire hazard.

Why is there this contradiction, therefore, in the external order and manifestation of modern Japanese city life? How is it that the traditional Japanese aesthetic seems to have been overpowered by the needs of twentieth-century man and the demands of his technological machine?

First of all, an interesting semantic detail: the Japanese write the words city, *shi*, and market, *ichi*, with one and the same ideogram. In other words a city is primarily a market place — a shopping centre. Western languages stress the rather abstract idea of a *civitas* (see *city*, *cité*, *citta'*, *ciudad* . . .): the totality of inhabitants and human activities. The Japanese language stresses the economic aspect: a city is a place where people do business, where goods are produced and exchanged.

If this point is kept in mind the physical disproportion and ugliness of Japanese cities does become more understandable; a certain logic links things together. A city is not meant to be beautiful, it is meant to be useful. Each new building that is erected — whether it be a five-storey concrete cube or a thirty-storey skyscraper, is an instrument for solving a specific practical problem. The city is the totality of these practical solutions. It is not a *civitas*, it is an *ichi*, a marketing thoroughfare.

Such clear focusing on the immediate problems of existence is typical of the Japanese pragmatic approach to life. Unlike the West, the roots of Japanese pragmatism do not spring from an academic basis; in effect they go back to the primeval intuitions of the people, to their most archaic values and ways of thinking. This world is not seen as the image of some more significant reality, but is absolute reality itself. Life, the most exquisite manifestation of being, is sacred and an ultimate good. Considered from this angle, pragmatism is not a philosophy hugging the earth, but a positive, often enthusiastic alliance with life. That is why Japanese cities may lack architectural harmony and balance but exude immense vitality and have so often a festive, even frivolous appearance. More than cities they are gigantic circuses, permanent world fairs, colossal merry-go rounds. Expo '70 and the Ginza-Shimbashi district of Tokyo were, after all, disturbingly similar!

The profound connection between Japanese ideas of beauty and nature is another factor worth looking into. Nature is divine, therefore nature is beautiful, and gardens are a form of worship. Japanese Shinto shrines are normally surrounded by tree groves, sometimes shrines have to be 'discovered' in deep, mysterious mountain recesses. Buddhist temples are quite often more famous for their gardens than for their buildings or art treasures. In other words, traditional Japanese ideals of beauty clash constitutionally with the brute reality of built-up space. If beauty is essentially nature, then a beautiful city, beautiful non-nature, is a contradiction in terms.

Apart from this the Japanese aesthetic has mostly idealized purity, simplicity, delicacy, intuition, suggestion, qualities which are difficult to combine with masses of buildings and vast crowds of human beings. The planning of beautiful cities requires

144

other canons, a certain anthropocentric boldness which is entirely foreign to Japanese culture — at least since Buddhism made its influence universally felt.

Japanese cities are almost exclusively composed of streets. One is invited to go, never to stop, sit, rest, contemplate. Space is indefinite. Nothing pulls it together, gives it a rhythm or a hierarchy of values. There are no squares, no pauses. When the central axis of a street lacks a concluding object — observes Yoshinobu Ashihara (*Exterior Design in Architecture*, 1970) the quality of space deteriorates towards the end. In a city where most streets have no 'concluding object' there must consequently be a deterioration of aesthetic space in all directions. But this is only logical. The utilitarian trading-centre city is meant for business, it is not a place to loiter or to look around. When business is over there are the amusement quarters for relaxation. A city is an instrument, not a background for ceremonies.

Yoshinobu Ashihara also rightly observes how the Japanese are extremely sensitive to the need for an internal order and the private secluded space of home, temple, inn, restaurant or theatre. This order stops more or less where shoes are put on. Beyond that point, an external, public order begins — and nobody, as yet, has ever cared much about that. A community, says Ashihara, is 'a mere collection of small internal orders'. Modern Japanese cities are confused because people lack the concept of 'an external order'.

During feudal times merchants were placed at the lowest level of the social scale. Could not some bygone shadows of negative discrimination still weigh on the city which was, after all and in great part, a merchants' creation and paradise? More importantly, a strict hierarchical society, in which authority percolated from above, did not encourage the development of cities as expressions of collective ambition. To build an Athens or a Florence needs the drive of independent city-states. Imperial Rome, too, it is often said, was really a glorified city-state; and Rome has been the model for Paris of later ages, and for most other western capitals.

Up until a few years ago Japanese cities were almost entirely built of wood. Even at best, wooden houses are not supposed to last more than a couple of generations. Earthquakes, fires, typhoons often destroyed them well before that limit of time. Necessarily a city must have appeared as something ephemeral, a conception which was surely encouraged by the Buddhist philosophy of impermanence. Under such circumstances it was difficult to think of a city as a vast structured organism monumentally surviving in time. The verb 'to be' sits solemnly on stone, marble and brick, but very flimsily on wood, paper, bamboo and plaster.

A final point. The rapid development of Japan since 1868 has involved both modernization — the adoption of technology and science — and westernization — the adoption of foreign values, tastes, ideals. Traditional Japanese cities may have offered views of a certain beauty. Ernest Satow described Yedo in 1867 as 'one of the handsomest cities in the Far East' (*A Diplomat in Japan*, 1921). The modernizing process brought new materials, new methods of construction and the ancient unity of style was immediately lost. 'The French Renaissance style was used in building a palace; a calm, half-timbered style for houses; the classical style for banks; the baroque for government offices; and the moorish for a museum' (Ino Dan, in *Western Influences in Modern Japan*, 1931).

Buildings constructed in the new fashion had to be first and foremost useful and were somehow freed, therefore, from all aesthetic constraints. This principle led to some curious results. On the one hand mediocre architects practised their profession believing in the popular view that 'if it is western it is necessarily ugly, so why worry'. On the other hand, men of intelligence could take advantage of an extraordinary freedom. They had no Parthenon clogging their vision. Experiments, sometimes bold, sometimes weird, took place everywhere. The skylines of Japanese cities, with their turrets and pinnacles, boxes, cubes and spheres, the infinite modern versions of the pagoda motif, looked more and more like those of a station on some outer planet in a science fiction novel. A genuine need for good taste in things western is now at last clearly emerging, and herein lies hopes for the future.

Will people so truly and traditionally enamoured with beauty put up with the present stringent urban asymmetry and imbalance for ever as a setting for their work and leisure? I feel confident that they will not. Lighting fixtures and fittings, for instance, were stark and shapeless thirty years ago. Now the standard of presentation and design is generally very high; it is sensitive, subdued, imaginative. Of course architecture and city planning are not simple. Japanese cities are no longer vast encampments of ephemeral huts: they are quickly solidifying into steel and artificial rock.

It is supremely important, therefore, that good ideas influence today's decisions for tomorrow. Ugliness petrified could be there as a punishment for generations to come.

Nō:
a search for the absolute

by Michel Random

One could say that a *Nō* performance begins and ends in the wings. From beginning to end it demands total concentration.

Nō performances are famous throughout the world for the extraordinarily slow pace with which the characters move and act. In fact, it is this very slowness which expresses the essence of *Nō*; that is, a concentration of energy in both attention and movement. 'Slow movement,' says the master, Manzanhuro Umewaka, 'is more difficult and much more demanding than rapid movement'.

The reason why *Nō* is so complex is simply because every element in it is reduced to the barest essentials. It is said that *Nō* is a poem performed as a chant or a dance, but how can we really define *Nō*? Zeami, without doubt the greatest master that the *Nō* theatre has ever known, wrote in the fifteenth century:

Forget the theatre and look at Nō
forget Nō and look at the actor
forget the actor and look at the idea
forget the idea and you will understand Nō.

It is not easy to understand the clues hidden in these words, which call to mind the spirit of Zen itself, since how can one speak of things which are always beyond the realm of words, except to describe what they are not? This is true of the *Nō* mask which is 'the expression beyond expression'. 'The actor must live behind his mask; the acting, however slow it may be, must appear to be spontaneous.' 'This is why,' says the master Umewaka, 'before an actor can really succeed in bringing out the beauty of *Nō*, he must be sixty or seventy years old'. Thus, apprenticeship must begin during childhood. This also helps us to understand why *Nō* actors hand down their teaching and their secrets from father to son.

The teaching of *Nō*, in fact, was secret up until 1909 when Zeami's basic work was discovered. This contained the secret tradition of *Nō* which could only be read by his closest disciples. For it was Zeami and his father, Kanami, who, towards the end of the fourteenth century, perfected a form of pantomime which was a development of the *sarugaka*, or popular theatre, and which was to become the *Nō* theatre.

In this famous book, Zeami developed the rules which lift the art of acting *Nō* to a sort of absolute perfection. It is a state in which the actor and even his acting cease to exist, to the point where a new level of being is achieved, the existence of which could not have been previously anticipated. This inexpressible state is compared by Zeami to a flower's perfume. The true connoisseur is aware of the moment when the actor becomes the embodiment of the character he is playing, so totally that it is as if he is inhabited by a new force. From this point of view, says Zeami, 'the connoisseur sees in his mind, whereas those who are not connoisseurs see with their eyes'. A true audience feels the emotional shock which is the extreme point at which the concentration demanded of the acting becomes unbearable. When this is reached, the actor makes a very rapid gesture to set himself free — as in the creation and release of a spark.

This unity of action is further emphasized by the fact that *Nō* has only one main character, the *shite*, meaning he who does or acts. He is assisted by a *waki*, a secondary character, and is accompanied by followers. The chorus comments, gives descriptions or takes over from the principal actor when he has to mime a long story. Lastly, the orchestra (which is first on stage) prepares the entry of the actor, supports his chant or that of the chorus, and provides the rhythm of the dance.

Everything is symbolic in *Nō* and, in every play, each gesture seems predetermined in minute detail. As a result of this, *Nō* audiences in Japan represent a very closely involved public, appreciating the smallest details of the scenes and studying the actor attentively to see how he will handle the difficult passages. The audiences are also able to read the most imperceptible movements. The handling of the fan, in particular, is one of the keys to appreciating the quality of *Nō* drama; depending on how it is held it can represent a shield, a sword, wine, water or a cup.

Touching the eye with the hand signifies weeping; the staff is a symbol of virility and dropping the staff can signify the lifting of a curse. It is surprising to note how far a carefully made mask, worn by an actor of great talent, can convey to the audience even the most subtle states of mind.

Moreover, a *Nō* play is constructed in such a way that, when the principal actor first appears, everything about him is immediately unusual. When the character enters, his strange gestures and words attract the attention of the other characters on stage — these are often monks. The monks immediately sense something not strictly human about the protagonist. They pose questions, therefore, to make the character talk and progressively reveal his true identity. And so, gradually, it becomes apparent that this strange character is a ghost.

It may be the ghost of an individual whose life did not end peacefully or that of a great warrior who lost his last battle and who has not achieved the serenity or rest to enable him to find ultimate peace. Or it may be the ghost of a woman who made a lover suffer torment and who, because of what she had done, met a bad end.

During the second part (after an interlude which features a short, self-contained farce or *kyogen*), the character returns in his true identity, which might be that of warrior, woman or demon. He acts out before the audience a scene of essential importance in his life. This scene contains whatever event is weighing heavily upon his soul. Sometimes he reaches a moment of frenzy, and it is precisely at this climax that he seeks to induce the monks to exorcize him by prayers, words, or asks the other people present to circle around him. Only then will his soul find the rest it needs to enter paradise.

The ultimate aim in *Nō*, paradoxical perhaps, is the achievement of naturalness. The actor must be so completely the embodiment of his mask and his character and must so project himself out of his own personality that everything appears to be perfectly true to life. Zeami says that once the techniques are mastered, 'the naturalness consists in returning to one's point of departure, but not completely, for there is a slight difference'. And *Nō*, doubtless, is just this slight difference.

Plate 31: Nō *performance.*

Plates 32-34 inclusive: *Images of contemporary Japan.*

Plate 35: *The fire-walkers of Takaoyama.*

148

4 Seen and heard

Water music
and white gloves

by Irma Kurtz

Each country has its own noises. England is tyres on a wet road and birds' song even in the centre of London; America is baseball commentary and frying food; France is wine being poured and swallowed and the spray of a perfume atomizer; Japan is the crunch of wooden soles on the gravel paths around the Meiji Shrine in Tokyo. There seemed to me something essentially Japanese about that sound which, at first, I found so puzzling, for I was unable to discover its source. There, on a lovely day in October, could it be the sound of a million diminutive drums being played with toothpicks, or the rustling leaves of a towering tree? But it was the sound of the Japanese themselves, of their wooden sandals on the gravel, the sandals of mothers bringing their beribboned children to be blessed at the shrine and fathers, bristling with cameras, and young people hand in hand strolling through the exquisite gardens. I remember, too, the endless rattle of ball-bearings in the Pachinko Parlour where what looked to me, I admit, like the world's most pointless game spills endlessly, purposelessly on. There was the noise of traffic — which in Tokyo really does roar as it roars nowhere else I can think of — and then the noise of that noise stopping suddenly on tiny back streets where shrines and wooden houses seem to have been living peacefully for ever. It is hard to forget hearing, most amazing, Handel's 'Water Music' pouring out of a 'Red Hot Jazz Club' in Shinjuku and the sound of a solitary cricket in Kyoto who lived outside the window of the bathroom where I drifted in hot water to my chin while it sang to me in what, for the moment, was the biggest and only voice in the world. That little cricket whose song I had read about in poems nearly a thousand years old, was an elegant cricket, a very old cricket, a very Japanese cricket.

Moreover, Japan smells good (despite the fact that its sewers stink). On a station platform near Mount Fuji the air smelled white, like snow, and in a small village miles from Tokyo the air was rusty, like turning leaves. Even in Tokyo, under the grey haze of car exhaust, there are spills of delicious scents: the powdery, ancient smell of the shrines, the leafy smell of the Japanese people themselves; and the provocative odour of food. Really fresh fish, grated horse-radish, cinnamon wafers, soy sauce, vegetables lightly cooked in broth — those tingling odours were a better advertisement for the countless restaurants in Tokyo than their windows full of extraordinary, highly-coloured plastic replicas of the food served within. I searched areas of Tokyo looking for the great source of these indigestible comestibles, but with no success; my mission was complicated by my inability to explain in Japanese that I was trying to find the plastic-food factory. Once, from the window of a taxi, I thought I saw a shop full of plastic ice-cream sundaes, but my driver, misunderstanding my excitement, hurled us even faster into the murderous Tokyo traffic.

I am still at something of a loss to explain exactly why I loved Tokyo from the first moment I saw it. No, the first sight of Tokyo was not beautiful, and all my interest did not blind me to the cars, the ubiquitous Coca-Cola signs, the haze, the unoriginal modern buildings towering too high, too far, too big. But then there was the driver of my taxi tapping one finger on the wheel in time to the Brandenburg Concerto which was playing on his car radio. Of course, it is dangerous to generalize, but three facts I give you which cannot be denied: it was a taxi; it was in Tokyo; I had never before been in a taxi anywhere in the world with Bach playing on the radio.

'*Hai*,' I said, for no reason at all except that it was my only word of Japanese.

'Nice music,' the driver said in English.

'*Hai*,' I said again, but with more confidence.

We rode the rest of the way to my hotel in companionable silence and, as we were of course caught in traffic on the motorway, I learned all I could about Japan from the back of his neck: the stiff, enviable black hair which the Japanese themselves so often and inexplicably denigrate; the ultra-conservative haircut; the collar of a scrupulously clean cotton shirt and, when he reached back to stretch, a highly-complicated and futuristic wrist-watch showing beneath the edge of his immaculate white gloves. The Japanese enjoy machinery and I suspect that the more dials, numbers and knobs on any appliance, the more it is appreciated. In the parks I used to watch long, silver aerials towering over clumps of trees and gliding along, it seemed, self-propelled; or perhaps the antennae of an odd Martian insect which always turned out, once clear of the shrubbery between us, to be a young man with an immensely complicated portable radio. Once I remember seeing six of these quivering filaments together over one clump of shrubbery; it turned out to be three young men with two immensely complicated radios each.

Tokyo is best seen from a height, for as there is a Tokyo life at street level, there is another, equally fascinating life, at the level of the lowest clouds. Every morning from my window on the twenty-seventh floor, I watched a dozen men on a neighbouring roof exercising to the rhythm of a big drum; the instrument was inaudible from behind my plate-glass, but I could see its sound perfectly well while the men bowed, lunged and swung their arms to its tempo. A few roofs away, under a net covering, some golfers practised their strokes — ambitious businessmen, perhaps, warming up for their social round on the green. A little way beyond, two teams of girls played at penthouse netball.

At night, Tokyo sparkles: the neon lights flicker in a strangely regular pattern and to stand above looking down at it is like looking down at the control panel of a vast, fabulous space-ship. I never dreamed that I would find in the neon light a new urban art form, but in Tokyo I certainly did just that; there is as much art in those bright pink and chartreuse lights as in the incredibly wrought garlands of paper flowers festooning the newly-opened restaurants, or the banners outside a small neighbourhood temple.

Every traveller develops a formula for learning about a city as quickly as he must in this jet-propelled age of ours. My own I call the 'pubs and public transport' method. I must admit that in Tokyo the second, public transport, led me rather quickly to the first; I never really knew what it meant to need a drink until I emerged, shaken, from the Tokyo underground at rush hour. The underground in Tokyo is rapid, well organized, cleaner than our own versions and nearly impossible for a westerner to find his way around in without some knowledge of Japanese. Only one of the difficulties is that many of the stations are vast complexes and if the traveller should stumble up out of the wrong exit he may find himself as much as half a mile from where he thought he was going to be. Mind you, he is in no real danger of starving or of any grave discomfort while he circles the underground looking for the right exit; at the largest stations, such as Shinjuku and Ginza, there is a whole subterranean city in full swing.

During rush hour nothing you have heard about Japan's grace or courtesy holds true; for an hour or so in the morning and an hour or so in the evening, the Tokyo underground is a seething phenomenon. Perhaps the best way to savour rush hour without actually enduring it is to pop down into any major underground station just after the worst of the press. There you need only look at the attendants, those who have just spent more than an hour pushing a solid wedge of humanity into the carriages; their haggard faces, collars askew, hats pushed back off sweating brows, their utter exhaustion tells you all you need to know of the Tokyo rush hour. Nor is it better above ground, where every street holds a necklace of cars strung like beads across the city, immobile, unchanging, petrified flies in amber. At certain hours it is advisable to allow as much as two hours for what would normally be a half-hour journey and at the worst hours I found it advisable to stay safely indoors, the way natives do on those tropical islands which are subject to brief, daily typhoons.

Markets are wonderful places where the most everyday items of local use are exotic marvels to the visitor. The endless covered market in Kyoto has a mood all its own. It is neither the Arabian Nights kind of the Middle East nor the bread-and-butter market of the North of England, although it has elements of both. It is a Japanese market and many of the most delightful things in it are tiny, or made of paper, or carved from thin wood. A shop window spread from top to bottom with fans could have been the specimen case of a giant lepidopterist; in a toy shop religious processions were carved in wood, each figure less than one inch high; an engraver sat behind his window full of nameplates and seals, and row after row of spangled and embroidered and printed scarves, dolls, posters, calendars, mugs, plates and banners (no doubt saying in Japanese 'Souvenirs of Lovely Kyoto'). Where the housewives shopped, that couldn't possibly be just food laid out so carefully and with such taste — those were treasures. Could those really be everyday oranges arranged in small baskets and counted out into golden groups of three? How many sorts of mushrooms can there be in Japan: when displayed in the Kyoto market I counted at least seven varieties exhibited like rare orchids on a blanket of green leaves? And what fish could feel despondent about being caught when it was to be shown in the market with all the pomp we would give to some Phoenician treasure dredged from an ancient wreck? A friend of mine from Marseilles, where they understand such things, once told me that you begin to judge the cuisine of a country (and in a Frenchman's case 'cuisine' means 'soul') when you see how the food is treated in the market-place.

I hold my Japanese memories with great care, all of them from the deep serenity of a Zen Buddhist temple to the laugh of a little girl who thought I was the funniest thing she had ever seen, while I was thinking that she was the most beautiful thing I had ever seen.

Abacus *by Tadashi Wada*

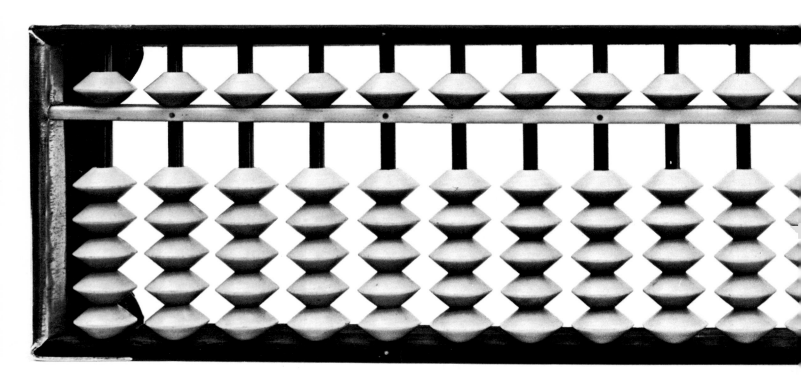

While the West awaits with awe and trepidation the relentless approach of the computer and its brave new world, Japan is countering the invasion with its own brain machine — the abacus (or, as the Japanese themselves call it, *soroban*). This mathematical calculator, originally invented thousands of years ago, was in use throughout the great early civilizations: Ancient Egypt, Persia and Rome are all known to have employed it. And in AD 600 the abacus found its way to Japan through the hands of Chinese merchants (thus *soroban*, from the Chinese for abacus, *suan pan*).

This ancient computer of the far eastern world consists of a compact wooden frame containing about thirty vertical rods, each holding one bead above the crossbar and four or five below. The bead in the upper section represents units of five, each of the lower beads a unit of one. Each vertical column, from left to right, represents a unit ten times more than that preceding it. Using this visual blackboard an abacus-user can add, subtract, multiply and divide with ease; indeed, an expert using it can accomplish square and cubic roots. Not only does the abacus fulfil the function of a desk-top calculator; its regular use flexes and develops the mind — for a fully trained abacus-user merely has to picture the device and mentally flip the beads to be able to produce immediate and accurate results to highly complex problems.

Banks, small businesses and housewives find the abacus indispensable, despite the flow of more 'sophisticated' machines into the country. At least, they thought they did, up to now. Recently a leading English language daily paper, the *Japan Times*, commented in its editorial: 'The sign of the times seems that the age of the *soroban* may be drawing to a close. There is a great deal of merit in the *soroban*. It is useful in training young minds. But the prevailing trend toward greater application of the machine in business is also a fact of life which must not be ignored.'

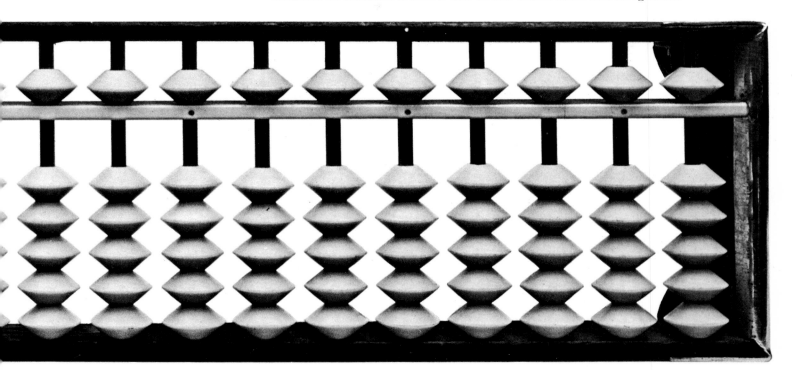

So the controversy smoulders on. 'Ancient abacus not taking back seat to computer,' announced a popular daily defiantly not long ago, attacking the Ministry of Education's decision to place less importance on the teaching of abacus to children. And the paper went on to point out that as the state schools' abacus lessons dwindle, so an ever-increasing proportion of children now attend private abacus tutoring after school hours. In Tokyo alone there are about 2,000 private abacus schools of every size straining to cope with the growing numbers of pupils. Although it is true that, for example, an abacus-trained clerk can expect faster promotion and a better salary, yet the pull of money does not entirely account for this upsurge of interest. The fascination of the *soroban* insinuates far deeper, appealing to a sense of mystery and magic. The national abacus champion of 1973, a housewife, appeared on television and amazed viewers with her supernatural skill in abacus calculation. With eyes closed, she was able to add up ten different ten-digit figures fired at her in rapid succession to produce a correct answer within a second of the final figure being put to her. One could call her a genius. But amongst Japan's younger generation this is no rare performance. The Japanese Chamber of Commerce and Industry sponsors official abacus examinations annually, and of one million people who take these each year, following a training of two or more years, about 5,000 emerge with first-class flying colours. But six months' to a year's training is normally sufficient to produce an abacus-user capable of solving simple business and household problems.

So, in an age of labour and time-saving devices, the *soroban* holds both material and mystic appeal. It has also achieved souvenir value: of five million abaci produced annually in Japan, 300,000 will find their way over to the United States, according to the Japanese Abacus Manufacturers Association. Whatever the future of the abacus on the business scene, one may be sure that it will never entirely disappear. The Japanese people would be loathe to lose an implement whose characteristic neatness, design simplicity and scaled precision are so akin to their own indigenous qualities.

Getting steamed up in Kyushu *by Charles Parr*

Between dripping palm fronds and trailing orchids a narrow path inlaid with cultured pearls snaked its way beside pools of clear water. A young girl came walking towards me and smiled sweetly as she passed. The fact that we were both undressed did not seem to bother her in the least, and oddly enough it did not bother me either. Like most visitors to Japan I had heard of the tradition of mixed public baths in Japanese hotels: this was my initiation. It was made easy by the fact that everyone around me was behaving with calm normality, as though nude bathing were the most natural thing in the world (as indeed it is).

This happened in Ibusuki on the southern tip of Kyushu in south-western Japan. I am convinced that several years ago a group of Japanese businessmen with unlimited funds summoned an architect and told him: 'Build an hotel. Make everything as big as you like. Have as much money as you want. However fantastic your plans — it's O.K. with us.' The result was the Ibusuki Kanko. Like the Empire State Building you cannot really believe it but it is undeniably there.

The foyer is gigantic — of cathedral proportions; walk another hundred yards or so and you'll find another just as impressive. The basement houses a department store, an enormous theatre, an amusement centre big enough to get lost in, and a tropical aviary. And if you picture the aviary as an outsize bird-cage a few paces across, you will, of course, be wrong. It is as big as a football stadium — all 109,000 square feet of it, and dense with vegetation.

But the star attraction is undoubtedly the 'Jungle Bath', also of enormous proportions and containing a whole series of steaming hot pools, including a sulphur bath, a seaweed bath, and soda, rose and jasmin baths, set amid a fantastic tropical decor with palm trees, bananas and exotic blooms flourishing in the humid warmth. It is available free to hotel guests, and one can spend a relaxing hour or so soaking in one bath after another. Ladies who don't wish to mingle have a separate pool of their own — in full view of the gents. Even this bathing complex does not exhaust all the possibilities, for outside on the beach one can stew gently in sand heated by underground thermal activity.

Kyushu (set roughly in the same latitude as Cairo) is semi-tropical in atmosphere and its thickly wooded countryside features palm trees, cedars and delicate bamboo. In no particular hurry, I chose to follow secondary roads, stopping every now and again to explore villages of blue-tiled wooden houses and sampled the local food at nearby inns, especially *mizutaki* — chicken cooked in a broth of ginger, soy sauce and *sake*. On several occasions I sent the car a mile or so ahead and walked in brilliant sunshine, enjoying the view in peace and meeting scarcely any traffic on the way.

Japan's 'tropical island' can be reached in less than two hours by air from Tokyo. Alternatively, if there's time to spare, one can take the Tokaido 130 m.p.h. 'bullet' train to Kobe and spend a whole day cruising through the Inland Sea to Beppu, and from

there make one's way south to Ibusuki along a delightful coastal route via Nobeoka and Miyazaki.

Kyushu is short on organised tourist 'sights' but strong on natural attractions, folk arts and handicrafts. The only popular and crowded centre is Nagasaki, where Japanese guides, each bearing aloft an identifying coloured pennant, lead coachloads of foreign tourists for the steep climb to the Glover House and the view across the harbour.

But get away from Nagasaki and Kyushu is all yours. To travel a whole day without passing another foreigner is a little unsettling at first, and it is true that there is occasionally some language difficulty, but this can be overcome with a dictionary, gestures and good humour. The comforting fact is that the people of Kyushu like foreigners — maybe because they see so few of them — and they will invite you home and feed you seaweed, rice and green tea at every opportunity. This happened to me on several occasions merely as the result of asking for directions in a village street. Incidentally, motorists on these country roads are exceptionally considerate and truck drivers will even pull up at the roadside to let you go ahead, bowing as you pass.

Local culture, rapidly dying in urban Japan, here survives intact. At Takachiho I climbed a hundred stone steps to a clearing among tall red cedars to witness an invocation to the Sun Goddess which has continued without interruption for at least a thousand years. Originally a pagan dance performed by local farmers to propitiate the Goddess and ensure good crops, it is now performed nightly at the Iwato Kagura Shrine, before an audience of several hundred Japanese sitting cross-legged on the matted floor. The dancers are still the farmers of the district and one of them, to whom I spoke through an interpreter as the audience were filing out, said yes, he thought it helped to get good crops, adding: 'We wouldn't feel safe without it'.

At Kamo, north of Kagoshima, pausing in a drive between paddy-fields in a valley with richly-wooded volcanic hills on either side, I saw a peasant boiling strips of oak bark in a huge vat. This turned out to be a two-man paper factory with a daily output of 80 sheets of beautiful parchment used mainly for religious inscriptions and despatched to shrines all over Japan. Work was immediately halted so that I could be shown the ancient procedure of washing, bleaching, pounding to paste, solidifying into sheets, pressing and drying. Kindness of this sort is almost embarrassing, since the tip which would be the easy way out almost anywhere else in the world is neither asked for nor expected by the country people of Kyushu (or for that matter, by the Japanese as a whole).

A little farther south I found the perfect answer to the 'What-shall-I-take-home' problem at the village of Miyama. Here a tradition of pottery-making has continued unbroken since the sixteenth century, when 80 Korean ceramists were brought back as prisoners of war. The ceramists are now in their 13th generation.

Thermal activity oozes, puffs, burps and belches all over Kyushu, with active volcanoes at Sakurajima and Aso — the latter with the world's biggest crater (the Ngorongoro crater in Tanzania would fit comfortably inside it) — plus boiling pools or 'hells' at Beppu and clouds of steam rising in every direction in the National Park in Unzen. Occasionally one comes across groups of Japanese soaking in open-air rock pools which are judged to be at the correct temperature for bathing (just below scalding it seems, when you first put a toe in).

However, a real glutton for punishment, I tried the sand-bath on the beach when I got back to Ibusuki, had myself buried alive by a female grave-digger, and dozed in warm steam until the tide came in. Before dinner, already an old hand at the game, I went for a further session in the Jungle Bath and afterwards strolled in that endless aviary.

People enjoying an open-air sauna bath on the beach at Ibusuki. Steam heat generated by natural thermal activity raises the temperature of the sand to a relaxing 90°F.

Setonaikai: the Seto Inland Sea *by John Grisdale*

The Setonaikai group of islands off the south-west coast of Japan (some authorities say there are over 700) are the legendary stepping-stones for Japan's ancient deities; their intrigue is heightened by the numerous coves and caves found amongst them — haunts and hunting grounds of smugglers and pirates in years gone by.

From Akashi Pier, a short haul from Kobe International Port in Hyogo Prefecture, I steamed by mono-class ferry with a Japanese friend and car in the mixed company of truck drivers (their diesels packed beneath) and a tangle of Kansai excursioners, to nearby Awajishima, the largest island in the Seto group (600 odd sq. kms). The temperature was topping 40 degrees Centigrade.

Awajishima is a fertile and undulating mass that swathed in a soft mist looked ethereal from the water as we approached. But for its bustling Iwaya Quay and the clutter on the waterfront, Awajishima appeared self-consciously, almost primly, clean and tidy. Fluttering pennants of washing blended oddly with masts of fishing smacks. Neat crimps of silver roofs bore a look of aged propriety.

Iwaya fishing village, its clusters of ancient cottages weathering the moods of a looking-glass sea while necklaces of sprats adorn sepia walls, is a marine artist's mecca. The air is impregnated with the compound aroma of *sake*, mackerel, pampano and eel.

Here, as everywhere in Setonaikai, the foreigner is a curiosity.

The island's balmy climate makes it ideally suited to flower cultivation. Daffodils, carnations, chrysanthemums and other species bloom abundantly in terraced greenhouses up neatly cultivated hillsides. As is the case everywhere in Japan, not a particle of land is wasted. The local flower farms and fish markets are mutual supports of the island's economy and both provide for the national needs of traditional cuisine and culture, notably *sashimi* (raw fish) and *ikebana* (flower arrangement). Such products find their way to department stores, *sushi* bars, plush restaurants and numerous flower arrangement schools in Tokyo and the provinces. Local trades also include roof tile manufacture and *sake* brewing.

Roads are good, and there are adequate gasoline stations, restaurants, shops and hotels. There is undoubtedly a great pleasure in motoring leisurely along a mini-Riviera coastline, passing a calm sea sprinkled with white fishing boats. Contrasts and contradictions are impressive: patchwork *futon* (eiderdowns) airing on sea walls, roped octopus jars piled against sea breakers, brash bowling centres, poem-engraved roadside memorials, vistas of green islets, grotto shrines, ferro-concrete *danchi* (flats). There is also the unique beauty of Keino Matsubara, a two kilometre-long National (beachside) Park homogeneously composed of pine trees twisting out of the pure sand but disfigured by a residue of littered camp sites.

According to Fishermen's Union officials, lounging at their Maruyama fishing village headquarters in cotton underwear and cooled by electric fans, the main bulk of local labour derives its living from the sea. But the sadness is that in ten years, the total fish yield has decreased by two-thirds due to mainland factory pollution of the fishing grounds.

The first day's drive terminated at the island capital's one-time castle (only the moat remains) town of Sumoto — focal point for holiday-makers and court trials. Sumoto is an idyllic rendezvous for bourgeois merchants and cartel salarymen who come from Kansai and the Kanto industrial centres. It has an air of mild opulence and acquired detachment, with western-style grand hotels and a charming yet expensive assortment of traditional *ryokan* (inns).

A plebeian alternative to the promenade sea-view suite, with its attendant facilities of water-skiing, speedboats, and horse-riding is local farmhouse accommodation. The one we tracked down, *Ohashi-so* (Big Bridge House), was tucked away among its own agrarian acres on a verdant hill overlooking west Setonaikai, the unpolluted part where the octopus is fresh as a sunrise. With free car parking, a steaming farmer's bath, a good breakfast and supper, the cost per person, minus beer, was really very cheap indeed. But, as we discovered later, even at a rustic farmhouse there is the risk of being subjected to the strident sounds of the discotheque; not to mention midnight revelry in the adjacent bathhouse so audible from behind paper slides.

Later, we made a fascinating one-hour trip in a crammed steamer from the small harbour town of Fukura, proud of its *Sazoe* ear shellfish, and traditional puppet theatre, to the famed Naruto Strait with its thrilling marine whirlpools.

The next island on our makeshift itinerary was Shodoshima ('small bean island') which we approached via busy and congested Takamatsu, capital city of Kagawa Prefecture on Shikoku Island facing Setonaikai.

Takamatsu is type-cast with all new urban growths in Japan. The only historic relic we saw was a small portside castle shrinking under tall office blocks around it. The business fraternity utilised the local airport extensively.

Landing at Shodoshima, we again chose farmhouse accommodation, on beach level, parking the car by a cabbage plot. Our stroll in the hot summer evening took us past coastal shopkeepers fanning themselves by the road and topless *obaasan* (old women) eating water melons in incense-filled shrines.

Shodoshima, 170 sq. kms in size and the second largest island in Setonaikai, is distinguished partly by its many 17th-century Edo Period soy sauce factories ('the life-blood of the Japanese') and its sixty-year-old olive groves ('rub olive oil into the navel and get younger' as the ad-men say). And then there is *somen*, a hair-fine hand-made noodle ('the longer you keep it the better it tastes'), popular in summer with tomatoes, shrimps, mushrooms and cucumber on ice — all dipped in a soy soup.

The historic industry of granite quarrying, which gives a war-battered look to much of the coastline, is still an important industry on the island. Granite can be seen gouged-out over a relatively large area. In olden times, the beige-coloured granite was used for military fortifications, notably at Edo (now Tokyo) and Osaka castles, but nowadays incorporated in hotel lobby pillars, mock fireplaces, tombs and campus statuary, etc.

A surprise item on our peregrinations through stunning scenery was located at the rock landscape of Kankakei. Here was the largest monkey colony of Japan. Its population of seven hundred was lorded over by a hairy red-faced boss-king named Danjuro IV after the distinguished *Kabuki* line of traditional actors.

Every spring since over 250 years ago, Shodoshima has seen a trail of Buddhist pilgrims circuiting on foot the 140 kms island road in seven days, paying homage at eighty-eight temples located around the island, walking in single file and wearing white *kimono* and conical straw hats, and tinkling silver handbells. They are said to be an impressive sight. Recently, *kamikaze* motorcyclist pilgrims have made noisy inroads into this walkabout tradition.

A further spectacular highlight in the Shodoshima calendar is the twice-yearly (15 April and 3 October) open-air performances of *Kabuki* drama by farmers at Hitoyama and Tonoshomaci. Young women who had to work in the industrial city of Osaka, rich in ancient culture, brought the old *Kabuki* and *Bunraku* (puppetry) theatre arts to the island many years ago. The Shodoshima stages, like *Nō* theatres, are under thatched roofs; the players enter by a long apron attached to the stage. Costumes, wigs, masks and make-up are in the rustic performances extraordinarily and superbly rich in design. Audiences sit on straw mats on the ground.

Finally, we reached Teshima, one hour on the ferry from the mainland and outside the compass of Japan's current industrial boom. The population is less than three thousand, mostly elderly people and married couples and children. There is a little dairy farming and a few olive and orange orchards. Young people and the ambitious migrate to the capitalist trade centres of Osaka and Nagoya to secure employment and a reasonable standard of life and rarely return. The island's educational facilities terminate at junior high.

The Setonaikai islands are undoubtedly rich in interest and fascination. There are the wide vistas of receding islands ever-changing in hue and tone with the sun's path; there are magical mists that transform tree-tufted hills and spurs into scroll painting idylls. The peasants who work the serrated fields up steep slopes, often with a baby strapped to their bent backs, are as tough as the fibrous roots of old pines clutching the cliffs. One senses a dogged devotion to a land-chain rich in legend and history, a sentiment that has of recent years manifested a near savage opposition to encroachments on traditional agrarian preserves by industrial prospectors. It is one of the tragedies of the technological advance that the once-pure seas of Seto are falling prey to problems of pollution — a far greater menace than the plunderers of its shipping lanes in years gone by.

Miyajima *by Geoffrey Bownas*

Itsukushima, or Miyajima as it is also called — an island in the Inland Sea fourteen miles to the Tokyo side of Hiroshima — is one of the three famous sights of Japanese tradition. The other two are Ama-no-hashidate, north from Kyoto on the Japan Sea coast, and Matsushima — the Islands of the Pines — near Sendai far to the north-east of Tokyo.

Miyajima — the 'Island of the Shrine' — is off the beaten track. In fact only the most determined of foreign travellers penetrate so far westwards. Not even the local Japanese 'farmers' cooperatives' on tour or factory group outings manage more than a four-hour stop-over on the island. The secret is to stay the night. Wave the last ferry passengers goodbye and, in utter calm, saunter back to your inn. That's what we did; a group of six of us, eager to experience a unique aspect of pure Japanese tradition.

Stripped of trippers and candy floss, the island suddenly reverts to its centuries-old colour and calm. The souvenir stall-keepers on the island's main street change gear abruptly and switch back to the demure reverence of bygone times. For this is a sacred island; so sacred that, in living memory even, it was kept inviolate from all forms of ritual impurity which included the dead and women in childbirth. Even today no islander is buried on the island, but on the mainland opposite; and family mourners remain there for ceremonial purification before their return. Such was the distate for blood-letting and the decay of death on the part of the three island deities, the daughters of *Susa-no-o*, the God of the Storm Wind, to whom the eighth-century shrine is dedicated.

Our inn was a two-storey building, utterly Japanese in style. The eaves of a thick thatch roof swooped outside our window, absorbing the glare of a midsummer sun and casting shade, a dappled light, across the *tatami* (straw matting) of our room. This was in the best native artistic traditions, for Japanese works of art and traditional design blend with and are enhanced by shadow; they lose their charm under the glare of direct light. Beyond the *shoji* (paper slides) just at eye level, a swift-flowing stream gorged into a waterfall, from dark pine-shaded rocks.

We had dinner in our room; the discreet tints of the plates blended with both food and the immediate surroundings and with the colours beyond the *shoji*. Later, we walked down towards the shrine of the island deities. Cicadas screeched, bullfrogs croaked raucously; somehow, the summer evening air was full, loaded, friendly. European summer nights, by contrast, seem starkly lonely. On the way, a floodlit pagoda soared out of a foundation of rustling bamboo. The shore was dotted with twisting pines, haphazardly planted with calculated design; for the Japanese landscaper shuns the order and symmetrical planning of his European counterpart; for him, not the logic of Rome and the Renaissance, but the intuitive, illogical rush of Zen.

At nine the next morning, we went back to the shrine. It was too soon for the day-tripping hordes. All six of us were seated solemnly on a low bench at the back of the dance stage which was roped round to restrain intruders from marring 'our' performance. To our left, there sat six musicians, three different drums, a reed and two plucked strings. Each musician wore the court dress of the thousand-year-old Heian age: silks blue-green, cream and violet. Beyond the stage, stretched the misty, turquoise sea, the red *torii* (gateway to a Shinto shrine) and deep purple hills of the mainland.

For thirty minutes, we were given our very own performance of the sacred *Bugaku*, a religious dance that came from China at about the time when the shrine was founded, late in the eighth century. The dancer wore a costume of dull scarlet, trousers long and trailing, his face hidden by a grotesque lacquer mask. He posed, arms raised at full stretch; he postured, strutted, paced the stage, pounding the floor with proud and pompous steps. Whenever an onlooker strayed beyond the rope and obstructed our gaze, everything stopped and the infiltrator was shepherded away. Then, as soon as the scene was clear again and my camera was seen to be ready, the music and dance recommenced.

We paid our fee, bowed our thanks to the dancer and musicians and took the cable car to the peak of Mount Misen. Three thousand feet below and stretching into the hazy distance, a myriad islets bobbled lazily on the misted Inland Sea. Behind us was a temple built, so they say, by one of the founders of Japanese Buddhism.

It's not at all easy to book a *Bugaku* performance. You must make advance arrangements and it is best to double check that the message has got through. And for three months from early July, there is no dance since the heat and dancer's sweat would damage the costume fabrics.

The Tokyo tourist headquarters never quite believed, I think, that a *Bugaku* performance could be booked. But, faced by a determined client, Tokyo phoned its local office at Hiroshima and our island hotel manager. For anything off the beaten traveller's track in Japan, anything that has not been done day in, day out for the past fifteen years, one must badger, insist. Sometimes this perseverance bears fruit and somewhere along the line, almost unawares, you find that the booking clerk, the tour adviser and the hotel manager begin to back you in a joint effort to defeat the system. You may discover finally, that Japan is perhaps the last land left in the world where service is a skilled, diligently learned and patiently practised profession. And for your pains, you may well be rewarded as we were with a unique Japanese happening.

Plate 36: *The* bugaku *dance of Miyajima.*

170

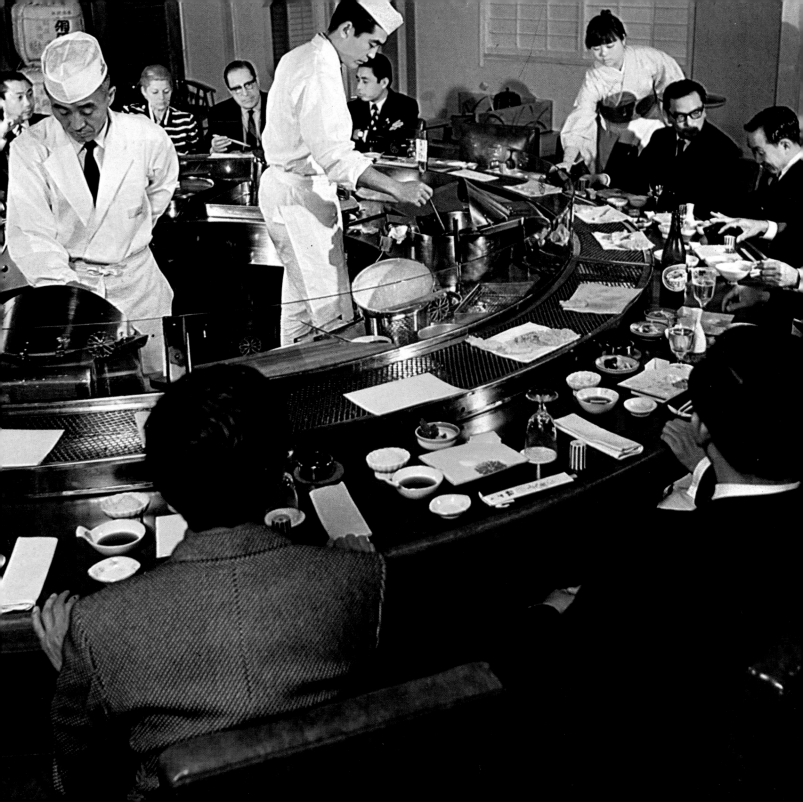

The Great Buddha of Kamakura *by Michael Cooper*

In 1195 Lord Minamoto Yoritomo and his wife Masako journeyed to Nara in central Japan to attend a dedication ceremony of the newly repaired Great Buddha, or *daibutsu*, statue at Todaiji temple. By that time Yoritomo was the virtual ruler of Japan. The rival house of Taira had been crushed in battle, the Emperor resided in solemn but powerless splendour in Kyoto, and Yoritomo, taking full advantage of his imperial appointment as *shogun*, or supreme military commander, exercised undisputed control over the country.

The enormous Nara *daibutsu*, still to be seen in its dusty immenseness in Todaiji temple, had been first constructed in the year 749, but fire and earthquake had periodically damaged the great statue. In 1180, during the military upheavals preceding Yoritomo's rise to power, the temple had again been razed and the statue partially destroyed. According to plausible tradition, it was during the re-dedication service in 1195 that Yoritomo hit on the idea of setting up a similar monument in Kamakura and thus increase the prestige of the city he had chosen as his administrative headquarters. But this ambition remained only a dream during the four remaining years of Yoritomo's life, and the unsettled state of the country after his death in 1199 prevented the quick fulfilment of the plan.

And so it was not until 1238 that the priest Joko managed to collect enough funds by public subscription to enable work to begin on a large wooden statue at Kamakura. The construction took five years, but finally, in 1243, the statue was completed and the dedication service was held. No records have survived describing this statue, and only five years after its completion it was severely damaged in a storm. As a result plans were drawn up to construct a new and more durable image of bronze.

After two failed attempts, the difficult work of casting was successfully concluded in 1252, and in the summer of that year, 53 years after Yoritomo's death, the great bronze statue of Amida Buddha — Lord of the Western World — was finally dedicated. Even by today's technical standards the accomplishment is highly impressive and one can only marvel at the skill and tenacity of the artists and workers involved in the enterprise. The statue was cast in separate horizontal sections with the utmost precision, and then the different parts were brazen together to form one large image. Workers then used metal files to make the join lines as inconspicuous as possible.

To say that the Kamakura *daibutsu* is a technical marvel is no exaggeration, yet the skill of the artisans who actually constructed the statue is surpassed by the expertise of the artists who designed it. For despite its height of 42 feet and its massive bulk weighing more than 100 tonnes, the Kamakura *daibutsu* possesses a far greater delicacy in features and workmanship than can be observed in its prototype at Nara. Furthermore, the Kamakura statue remains to this day just as it was when finished in 1243, whereas the larger Nara *daibutsu* has been patched and repaired so often that little of the original metalwork has survived.

An outstanding feature of the Kamakura *daibutsu* is the skill with which its designers calculated the dimensions of the seated figure. To maintain the appearance of correct proportion in any large structure some distortion must be introduced so that the viewer receives a balanced visual impression. Thus, when seen from behind or from the sides, the Kamakura statue appears as a grossly round-shouldered figure with

Plate 37: *The Great Buddha of Kamakura.*

Plate 38: *A tempura bar.*

175

an over-sized, top-heavy head. But no trace of this distortion is apparent when the statue is viewed from the intended vantage point, that is, about five yards from the front of its base. Seen from this viewpoint, the *daibutsu* looks down benignly on pilgrim and tourist alike, giving the impression of perfect visual balance and proportion.

The delicate features and graceful design of the great metal statue are particularly noteworthy. The loving Amida Buddha is depicted in serene meditation, an inspiration and source of strength for the Buddhist faithful beset by the trials and sufferings of human life. According to Buddhist teaching, man must place his complete trust and faith in the saving efficacy of the all-compassionate Amida Buddha, and the Kamakura statue, with its calm, serene expression and its hands joined in meditative prayer, seems to epitomize the spiritual strength and infinite love of the Lord of the Western World. The impression of peaceful recollection is accentuated by the rhythmic, symmetrical folds of the robe. Not only the design of the robe but also some of the facial features reflect Greek influence, which indirectly reached Japan via China and Korea long before the Europeans first came to Japan in the middle of the sixteenth century.

The *daibutsu* was originally housed in a large wooden temple, but fire, storm and earthquake repeatedly damaged the building. The site of the statue is only a mile from the shore of the Pacific Ocean, and, in 1495, a tidal wave inundated Kamakura and swept away the temple building. Since that time the statue has remained seated placidly in the open air, exposed to sun and rain, frost and snow. Still to be seen dotted around the statue are the large foundation stones on which the wooden pillars of the temple once rested. Voices have been raised during the past four centuries suggesting the reconstruction of the temple, but few would deny that the natural setting of the statue greatly enhances its beauty, and it is unlikely that the *daibutsu* will ever again be boxed up within the cramping confines of a building.

The first westerner to visit the statue and record his impressions in writing was the Englishman, Captain John Saris, who passed through Kamakura while on his way to Edo, modern Tokyo, to pay his respects to the *shogun*, Tokugawa Hidetada, in 1613.

'We saw many Fotoquise *(hotoke)* or Temples as we passed, and among others one Image of especiall note, called Dabis *(Daibutsu)*, made of copper, being hollow within, but of a very substantiall thicknesse. It was in height, as wee ghessed, from the ground about one and twentie or two and twentie foot in the likenesse of a man kneeling upon the ground, with his buttockes resting on his heeles, his armes of wonderfull largenesse, and the whole bodie proportionable, he is fashioned wearing of a Gowne. This Image is much reverenced by Travellers as they passe there. Some of our people went into the bodie of it, and hooped and hallowed, which made an exceding great noyse.'

Today, just as in Saris' time, it is still possible to enter the giant statue and inspect the rough-finished cavernous interior.

In more modern times there has been no lack of reports written by foreigners who have made the journey to Kamakura and visited the famous statue. Perhaps the most perceptive of all these accounts was written by the learned Basil Hall Chamberlain, who lived for many years in Japan and became an acknowledged expert in its culture.

Far from palling, repeated visits to the *daibutsu* reveal hitherto unnoticed beauty and deepen one's appreciation of this great statue seated placidly and serenely for more than seven centuries in the Kamakura valley near the ocean. In the hectic rush of contemporary life in Japan, with its jet planes, Bullet Train and ceaseless whirling computers, the calm and peaceful image of Amida Buddha has surely a relevant message for modern man.

Cormorant fishing spectacular *by Tony Dyson*

For centuries men have trained animals and birds to help them hunt for food or simply in the pursuit of sport. In Japan one of the most unique teams must be that of the cormorant and the local fishermen of the Uji and Nagaragawa rivers, who, working at night with the aid of burning braziers, provide onlookers with a remarkable fishing spectacular.

Cormorant fishing has been practised in Japan for well over a thousand years, and chronicles written around the year 900 describe how *ayu* (fresh-water trout), caught by cormorants, were regularly presented to the court at Kyoto and much enjoyed by the feudal lords. From this time on the cormorant fishermen received special privileges from the ruling classes, and rivers which they fished were protected by Royal Charter.

This traditional form of fishing (known in very few places outside Japan except perhaps on the River Conway in North Wales) has survived in only two places in Japan, one near Kyoto and the other in Gifu. Although hardly a commercial proposition, it persists as a tourist attraction in much the same way as it has always done. The poet Basho writing about cormorant fishing in 1866 clearly refers to the sport as a tourist attraction. The cormorant season lasts from mid-May to mid-October.

Although there are four different species of cormorant found in Japan (River, Sea, Princess, and Island), the sea cormorant is used almost exclusively for this type of fishing. The Japanese fishermen find this species preferable to the others because they are the largest and strongest birds and therefore able to be worked harder, and also because of their particularly mild temperament.

Wild cormorants which breed on the coast of Ibaraki Prefecture, about 200 miles north of Tokyo, are caught during the winter months when they are lured down on to the rocks by decoys set by the fishermen. The first birds caught are used as additional decoys for catching others. Immediately they are caught a thread is carefully stitched into the cormorant's two lower eyelids then drawn up over the bird's head and tied. This process effectively covers the eye with the under-lid thereby temporarily blindfolding and calming the bird.

The birds are washed in warm water then daubed with a mud paste which, when dried, flakes off removing dirt and insects from their feathers. This cleaning and calming procedure is repeated several times until the fishermen feel that it is safe to remove the thread binding the eyes.

The feathers on one wing are clipped to prevent the birds from flying and the beak trimmed since its normal razor sharpness would be a danger to the handlers during training.

During the first few days after capture the trainers try to keep as close to the birds as possible, frequently removing them from their bamboo cages, four birds to a cage, and gently rubbing their heads and bodies to get them accustomed to being handled. It takes at least two weeks for the birds to feel at home in fresh water, and as they do not usually catch any fish themselves during this time they are fed with fresh water fish by their trainers. Set to work alongside older birds they soon seem to adjust to their new environment.

Although it takes over two years to train cormorants for this work the birds usually live to about twelve years old, giving them a working life of about eight years.

There are two different types of cormorant fishing: the first where the birds are allowed to swim free, this system usually being chosen when they are fishing in lakes or other still water, and the second more widely known method where the birds are controlled by the fishermen with light lines tied round their necks. The lines are tied in such a way as to allow the birds to swallow the smaller fish they catch but prevent the larger ones from passing down the gullet, the bird retaining these in its throat whilst diving for more. After the bird has caught three or four large fish it is brought back to the boat and made to disgorge them.

The accompanying sightseeing boats accommodate between twelve and twenty people, and are laden with traditional food, including broiled *ayu,* as well as unlimited supplies of *sake* and beer. Fireworks, an important part of the festivities, are on sale from small boats moving up and down. On the bows of the fishing-boats are hung flaming braziers of pine logs, the light from which attracts the fish to the surface. It produces the effect of a glorious fairytale tableau.

The boats, about forty-five feet long and constructed of Chinese black pine are manned by four people. The master fisherman, or *usho,* and his assistant who control the birds both wear traditional costume comprising a long grass skirt over a blue tunic and a blue turban-like hat whilst the other two people control the boat, one from the stern and one from the centre.

In one evening, each bird will catch about forty or fifty fish, but it is not unknown on exceptionally good nights for them to catch in excess of a hundred. A big enough catch to feed a feudal lord and his retainers, or more especially the gourmets patronising the finer restaurants in today's big city centres.

5 Food and wine

Feast of food by *Jill Gribbin*

Of all the world's great cuisines, Japan's dishes must be the most elegantly simple. It is the taste for natural things, of course, which is the essence of Japanese culture. Japanese tradition prefers pottery to porcelain, soft reed mats to carpets, iron to bronze and wood to ivory. In such ways, despite superficial borrowings from Chinese culture, Japan differs from her great Asian neighbour.

Pure Japanese cuisine, too, is also highly idiosyncratic, although there are detectable influences from Korea. Why the Japanese people, their culture and their cuisine should be so distinctive remains something of a mystery.

The staple foods of Japan are rice, soy beans, fish and seaweed. Every traditional Japanese meal uses all these ingredients in some form: soy beans are fermented into bean paste *(miso)*, salted and boiled, sweetened and mashed, turned into the light and delicate Japanese soy sauce *(shoyu)* and formed into a creamy bean curd *(tofu)*. Rice apart from being the food of life to the Japanese — the word for cooked rice, *gohan*, also implies 'a meal' — is also the basis of *sake*, the Japanese rice wine, and its sweetened form, *mirin*.

Fish is so abundant in Japanese coastal waters that even the introduction of meat in the latter half of the 19th century did not diminish the importance of fish to the Japanese diet. Raw fish and shellfish, one of the greatest of Japanese delicacies, demands perfect freshness; not unnaturally the amazing efficiency of the Japanese fishing industry is hard to equal anywhere in the world; fish to be eaten raw is never frozen, even during the intolerable heat of summer. A Tokyo fish shop delights all the senses. Dried bonito *(katsuo)*, a fish from the mackerel family, is a basic ingredient of the *dashi*, the distinctive Japanese stock, together with dried kelp *(konbu)*. Other varieties of seaweed are used for wrapping balls of rice (as with *sushi*) as an all-purpose flavouring and as a vegetable in soup.

An essential part of every Japanese meal is the ubiquitous green tea *(o-cha)*. It is a tea that comes in a great many varieties, classed according to the size of the leaf, where it is grown and whether or not it has been smoked. Indeed, such is its appeal, complexity and promise that it has evolved its own connoisseurs who exhibit the same passionate concern for taste and bouquet as connoisseurs of French wines.

Then, there is powdered tea which is made into an elusively satisfying brew for the tea ceremony and is used as a flavouring for sweets. A green tea-flavoured syrup poured over crushed ice is a traditional and cooling summer treat.

Vegetables are also very important to the Japanese diet. The variety of vegetables grown in Japan today is astonishing and includes Irish potatoes, sweet potatoes, yams and Jerusalem artichokes, firm 'English' tomatoes and the fleshy Mediterranean kind, white cabbage, red cabbage, Chinese cabbage, broccoli and sprouts, spinach and kale, pimentoes, celery and asparagus. The indispensable, traditional vegetables, however, are the thin Japanese leek *(negi)*, a giant white radish *(daikon)*, Chinese cabbage *(hakusai)*, lotus roots and shoots, aubergine, Japanese horseradish *(wasabi)*, edible chrysanthemum leaves, burdock, bamboo shoots, spinach, root ginger, many varieties of aromatic mushrooms, edible ferns, peas and beans.

Fruit in Japan is abundant, and includes many fine varieties of apples and pears, grapes (made into a variety of drinkable and not-so-drinkable wines), plums, cherries, melons — including an abundance of watermelon — and two crops a year of delicious strawberries (one of them being in January!). But most typical of Japan are the varieties of fragrant orange, including the sweet 'mandarin' orange *(mikan)*, and the golden persimmon which seems to grow in everyone's back yard from the north of Honshu to the southernmost point of Kyushu.

Very little is known about the Japanese diet in very early times but chronicles of the mediaeval period suggest that it barely changed until the widespread introduction of western food and cooking methods in the middle of the 20th century (post 1945). Today's Japanese, however, is a good judge of pizza, hamburgers and steak. It is worth noting, too, that the Japanese way with salads is a wonderful inventive blend of American dash and Japanese delicacy, and it also goes to show how all western food in Japan becomes touched, however lightly, with a Japanese flavour.

Although the traditional Japanese diet was not only rather frugal but also low in protein — a contributing factor to the slight build and sallow skin of the Japanese people until recent years — it was not, however, lacking in vitamins and minerals. And with the modern addition of much larger quantities of meat and fish the Japanese diet is now an extremely healthy one.

A typical office worker's day begins with a hearty breakfast of rice, soup, vegetables, seaweed and raw egg (although boiled eggs and toast are becoming increasingly popular). He will eat a large bowl of noodles at mid-day, a hot snack at around six o'clock, probably delivered to his office, and a family dinner when he finally arrives home.

The great number of restaurants in Japanese towns catering for different kinds of Japanese meals and snacks, not to mention western food, is one of the wonders of Japan. Traditional restaurants have an apprenticeship system similar to that in the French tradition, leading to the star rôle in the kitchen, the *ita-mae*, literally he who stands before the chopping board. His most important attribute, by which he is recognized, is his skill with the knife, or, more accurately, the range of knives each with its own use, that are usually found in the Japanese kitchen. It is said that it is possible to recognize an *ita-mae* from the pattern left by his knife on the cut edge of a *daikon*.

The care taken in the preparation of Japanese food, whether at home or in a professional kitchen, is not only spiritually satisfying; it is also highly practical. Good Japanese cuisine demands that the food should be absolutely fresh and of the highest quality possible — there are no thickened sauces to cloak any slight loss of flavour.

Fortunately, unlike Chinese food, virtually all Japanese dishes can be prepared in advance and served at room temperature, the only regular exception being soup and the 'one-pot' dishes such as *sukiyaki*. The meal usually begins with a prolonged course of appetizers accompanied by *sake*, which is no longer drunk once rice appears on the table. Appetizers might be such things as quail eggs, roe, broiled vegetables or fish, fish paste, steamed chicken or game, or raw fish. The next 'course' is a setting of side dishes and soup. The side dishes include a boiled dish, usually vegetables, a serving of meat or fish which has been braised or grilled, and a small dish of raw vegetables or fish dressed with vinegar or pounded sesame seed. The meal is invariably concluded with a bowl of rice, some pickles and green tea. All manner of courtesies and rules are quoted on the subject of eating Japanese meals but other than in extremely formal company the dishes may be eaten in any order. Casual family meals often omit the appetizer course and consist simply of two or more side dishes with rice and soup.

Sushi *by Wendy Hughes*

'*Irasshai!*' — a welcoming shout from half a dozen lusty throats as my host, Yamaguchi-san pushed open the sliding wood and glass door of his favourite *sushi* haunt. Inside the shop just off Tsukiji, Tokyo's wholesale fish market, there stood in full view a glass-fronted refrigerated cupboard running the length of the counter, liberally stocked with succulent slabs of red, white and pink fish, orange caviare and shellfish of every shape and colour. And behind laboured a team of *itamae-san* — young men in spotless white overalls, their brows ringed by a twisted band of towelling *(hachimaki)*. While keeping up a constant, boisterous conversation with their customers, breaking off periodically to join in with the general shout of welcome each time a customer entered, the *itamae-san* continued moulding their *sushi*. With lightning movements they would shape a mound of vinegared rice into oblong mouthfuls: a soupcon of *wasabi* (vivid green horse-radish sauce) and a sliver of red, white or pink fish, a slice of *tamagoyaki* (sweetened and folded fried egg) or a glossy pink *ebi* (prawn) — et voilà.

Western palates have generally never experienced the joys of raw fish and tend to turn pale at the thought. To the initiated, however, there are two forms of raw fish — *sashimi* (snippets of raw tuna and cuttlefish) and *sushi*.

To begin with, Yamaguchi-san ordered three *sushi* each, 'of the best *toro*'. (*Toro*, it seems, is the best and richest cut of the tuna fish.) Instantly, with stunning expertise, six slivers of pink fish were sliced from the slab of fish with a *hocho* (meat cleaver), and moulded on to the rice mounds. And there were three miniature culinary masterpieces grouped ready to eat. No chopsticks here; connoisseurs always use their fingers to pick up a slice, flip it fishy side down into a saucer of *murasaki* (soy sauce is never called *shoyo* in a *sushi* shop) and deposit it effortlessly, upright once more, into their mouths. Not so an amateur like myself. But my trail of soy sauce from saucer to mouth was politely ignored. Surprisingly, the taste was not fishy as one would imagine, nor was the texture chewy. It was like eating avocado or mushroom — effortless and exotic.

From that moment, I was tempted with trios of every variety of *sushi* the house could offer. *Maguro* (the red cut of tuna) was followed by delicate fragments of ice white *ika* (cuttlefish), watermarked *tai* (sea bream), orange *akagi* (ark-shell), tiny pieces of *norimaki* swathed in seaweed and stuffed with *maguro* or cucumber (the final appearance resembling that of savoury liquorice allsorts). There were gobbets of *ikura* (orange caviare) of giant proportion and maroon-frilled *tako* (octopus) interspersed with curls of pink *gari* (ginger).

Customers seated at small tables in the shop were being served with black lacquer boxes filled with exquisitely arranged *sushi*. These, contrary to all elaborate appearance, were the management's budget set meals, priced according to the quality of the fish used and the proportion of fish to rice. At the counter, however, customers were free to select from the higher quality cuts of fish which had been haggled over in the Tsukiji fish market that morning.

Finally, we sipped mugs of scalding green tea and were later handed *oshibori* — the steaming hot towel for the refreshment of guests offered everywhere in Japan.

Sukiyaki *by Yvonne Whiteman;*

Sukiyaki — most robust of Japanese dishes — is the outstanding exception in a culinary tradition that makes relatively little use of meat. To a Westerner this simmered beef dish epitomizes Japanese cuisine, but for a Japanese family such luxurious fare is a far from everyday speciality. The sukiyaki tradition is still young, for until the Meiji Restoration of 1868 Buddhist convention forbade the eating of beef and pork. But the western custom of meat-eating soon found its way to Japan, on whose pastureland magnificent cattle are now reared (notably the Matazaka breed, into whose hide beer is carefully massaged some days before slaughter, to produce the soft flesh much prized in sukiyaki cooking). Today's sukiyaki is something of a hybrid. We think of it exclusively as a beef dish, but as a method of cooking it can apply equally well to chicken or pork: the name originally meant 'grilled on the blade of a plough'. Farmers and huntsmen out in the wilds killed and cooked their meat over an open fire, on whatever utensil happened to be available — usually a ploughshare. But sukiyaki is a misnomer nowadays, for *yaki* refers to grilled foods, and the dish we eat now is anything but grilled. In fact, it straddles two categories of Japanese cooking: *nabemono*, which applies to dishes cooked at the dining table, and *nimono*, which means boiling in seasoned liquid.

The meal itself is leisurely — deceptively informal — scaled down to a moment by moment aesthetic appreciation of arrangement, savour and flavour. To begin with, an appetizer. Your hostess serves you deftly, almost invisibly, with perhaps a thimbleful of chicken; a lettuce oval; a tenderly browned cube of bean curd and two crossed strips of cuttlefish grilled in soy sauce: a veritable culinary landscape on its curved rectangular raised plate. Then, possibly *miso* (soya bean) soup — fragrant curls of seaweed, diminutive cubes of bean curd and transparent emerald rings of spring onion set against the rich sienna background of the porcelain soup bowl. And the warmed *sake*, needless to say, flows in plentiful supply.

A heavy iron pan melting with beef fat appears on a small stove on the table. Why do the Japanese prepare sukiyaki in front of you? They say that it is more relaxing and hospitable; that you can see what you are getting; that you can select what you want when you serve yourself. I prefer to believe that sukiyaki is one of Japan's love philtres, set to lure all unwitting tourists into an epicurean trance of fascination.

The first piquant aroma of beef and soy sauce curls into the already heady air — wafer thin slivers of beef surrounded in their simmering pan by lettuce, bean curds, transparent noodles, leeks and mushrooms. Side plates are grouped before you: radishes, gherkins and chopped cabbage; fluffy rice heaped in its bowl. Finally, about fifteen minutes later, at the peak of expectation, the feast is offered to you. Soy sauce above to add poignancy, whipped raw egg below to cool and cream the sizzling beef, sugar added to taste — need I say more? Conversation dwindles to a shapeless murmur as the chopsticks rise and fall, while the *sake* flasks are refilled and the second, third . . . and fourth helpings of sukiyaki are served. It is not surprising that the sukiyaki house has now established itself firmly in the Japanese gastronomic tradition, alongside the sashimi restaurants and tempura bars. Sukiyaki has indeed come far from the days of the ploughshare.

Tempura *by James Goodall*

'Do you like fish?' inquired my host. I hesitated. Limited though my knowledge of Japanese food was, I knew that 'fish' could well mean raw fish *(sushi)* and I wasn't sure whether eating raw tuna, even though it was caught that morning, was going to inspire the initial confidence I needed in my desire to explore the full range of Japanese cuisine. My momentary indecision communicated itself immediately to my companion. 'I was thinking of fried fish; what we call *tempura*,' he added. 'If that suits you we'll go to a tempura bar.'

And that's exactly what it was — a bar around which one sits on high stools facing the chef who creates his delicacies under your nose and before your very eyes. This involvement with the chef is an essential part of a tempura meal as one is meant to observe the quality of the food about to be cooked and stimulate the appetite by taking in the cooking aromas.

There was a lot to look forward to. According to the translation on the particular tempura bar menu, we were about to be served shrimps, prawns, sillago, conger, goby, white-bait, squid, shell ligament, crab meat, oyster, mushrooms, gingo nuts, egg plant, ginger root and bell peppers. All exquisitely fried.

As we sat down, a waitress in *kimono* supplied us with an enormous bib or napkin that covered one's front from the chin downwards and spread over the knees. Almost imperceptibly she ties it on with ribbons from the back. My host then checked the menu and had a brief conversation with the chef. The sillago, oyster and ginger root weren't available tonight but would I like to take part in the rest of the menu? It all sounded exceedingly good.

Within minutes, the waitress returned and set out before us on a tray a series of bowls (I counted five) and other assorted stoneware. There was no disguising the *sake* bottle and cup and so, according to custom, we poured each other's drinks and continued to do so throughout the meal. Also set out was a small dish containing slices of lemon and some salt, a bowl containing radish puree and a large pot of soy sauce. 'You have a choice of sauces,' observed my host. 'You can either squeeze the lemon and mix it with a little salt or you can pour some soy sauce over the radish and use that. They both improve the taste of the food.'

We downed another cup of *sake* and the chef broke several eggs into a large bowl and began whisking the contents vigorously. This was evidently one of the secrets of successful tempura cooking — producing a batter that was of the highest quality. Each chef has his own recipe — which is his own secret. Frying oils that can be used include sesame oil, rape-seed oil, salad oil, torreya nut oil and olive oil.

All around the bar was a smaller raised ledge. Placed on it in front of each customer was a paper doily. Upon this doily with the hand of a magician our chef deposited the first sizzling tempura delicacy. A large prawn. 'Now take hold of it with your chopsticks,' said my companion, 'dip it into the sauce of your choice and take a small bite. Not too much because it will be very hot.' As splendid as British fish batter might be, the sheer transparency and lightness of this creation was something to revel in in itself. And so followed a whole assortment of fried fish, shell-fish and vegetables and a number of bottles of warm *sake*. An hour or so later we reached the end of the menu. 'Now,' said my host, 'it is customary to select one or two of the dishes you enjoyed most and the chef will repeat them for you.' More shrimps and mushrooms.

But even after the second helping of this delectable fry-up the feasting wasn't over. At this point the waitress returned again, this time presenting us with a large bowl of rice and a selection of pickled vegetables by way of a salad. In the salad dish were portions of pickled sliced radish, cucumber and cubed stems of radish. All rather strong but, seemingly, a good digestive. Finally, almost as a crescendo to this two-hour banquet, I was invited to partake of a large bowl of shell-fish soup seasoned with soy sauce. As I raised the bowl to my lips I could almost see the waters of the Sea of Japan; not unnaturally I could identify the ozone.

Tea, of course, actually concluded the ceremony, for that in a sense was what it was. One had eaten well and greatly enjoyed what must be the nearest to western cooking there is in Japan. But one had also been through an experience and for the gourmands of this world that is of the essence; it is also essentially the quality of Japan.

Saké _by Nobutoshi Hagihara_

'Commander Bond, you are remarkably civilized — for a European,' observed the particularly scrutable Japanese chief of police, after James Bond congratulated him for serving _sake_ at the right temperature — 98.4°F exactly.* James Bond, of course, did not know what he was talking about, but his host was too civilized to tell him that.

*_You Only Live Twice_

Sake — Japanese wine brewed from rice — has been produced since earliest times, probably dating back to the beginning of rice cultivation itself around 400 BC. It is also known as _hyakuyaku-no-cho_ — the best of one hundred medicines. At one time it was considered a purely sacred drink, a ritual offering made to the _kami_ (gods) on festival days by young virgins. On these occasions the girls produced the _sake_ themselves by chewing the rice. This process, known as diastase, turned the starches into sugar so that fermentation could follow. This practice still survives at certain shrines. Today, _sake_ — the national drink — is, of course, taxed (it is an important source of revenue) and production is strictly controlled by the government. Alcohol percentage varies between 15 and 22. The standard yeast fermentation process is unique to Japan — the climate playing no small part in its success.

A noble survivor from Japan's extraordinary past, _sake_ is, perhaps, the only one which still has meaning in the everyday life of the Japanese. One is sometimes tempted to think that other relics such as traditional gardens and tea ceremony — which continue to attract foreigners to Japan (and sometimes the Japanese themselves) — have become no more than museum pieces following the relentless westernization which Japan has undergone. But whatever the truth of that, _sake_ is alive and fairly well. It has been having a hard time, of course, what with the rivalry of beer, wine, whisky and brandy; and the struggle is not over. One of the more regrettable consequences of all this is that manufacturers have tried to popularize the taste of what was once an invigorating drink, and have introduced flashy bottles and trendy _sake_ containers, which are quite alien to the _sake_-drinking tradition. However, if you go for the small locally produced products, rather than the leading brands, you will discover the true dry, silky, tender taste of authentic _sake_.

In spite of the many attempts to commercialize and popularize this unique drink there are plenty of Japanese who will only take the real thing. _Sake_, for example, is the most appropriate drink for an elegant feast with _geisha_ in attendance. At the other extreme it is still common to see Japanese workers on their way home in the evening standing to drink at the _sake_ stalls or shops, rather like the Englishman who drops in for a quick pint at his local before dinner. In this, as in other respects, and in other countries, it is the classes at the two ends of the social ladder who join hands in taste and inclination. It is left to the so-called middle classes to patronize the notoriously expensive Ginza bars, where the expense-account drinker joins the customers and hostesses for whisky, brandy or even beer — but never _sake_.

Perhaps the reason is that _sake_ is ideal with Japanese food, which one certainly won't find in a Ginza nightclub. But there is a more basic reason, for which the guide books and James Bond must take some of the responsibility. They all insist that _sake_ must be drunk hot, and in doing so have helped to deceive not only foreign visitors, but also the middle-class Japanese, who are often too anxious to believe what foreigners tell them. Consequently, foreign liquors have established themselves as 'easy drinks', involving no nonsense about warming to the right temperature or serving with the appropriate ceremony (something which would appeal to the more liberated women of Japan). But the plain fact is that *sake* can be drunk and appreciated either warm or cold, according to taste and convenience. Did the old *samurai* have the time or opportunity to warm their *sake* before going out to fight?

Sake, in fact, is as easy to drink as any convenience liquor from the West, which means that you can drink it when you like: before, during or after meals. But this poses another problem: the more pretentious Japanese will continue to ignore it as a drink because it lacks sophistication. *Sake* is in this sense really up against it; the authentic and the sophisticated rarely go together, and though Japan wants both, she has spent a hundred years preferring the second to the first. Even the Japanese Imperial family was accustomed, when elder statesmen or other VIPs were seriously ill, to send them a present of wine or champagne, but never *sake*. Yet *sake* is also a divine or ritual drink, like wine in Christianity. It is indispensable to Shinto, of which the supreme guardian has always been the Imperial family. Has the awe been lost as well as the pretence of sophistication? Not yet, perhaps. During World War II the ordinary soldiers of Japan exchanged cups of *sake* before a battle; and even today the *Nō* actors drink a ritual cup before the performance of their mystic drama.

Authenticity and ritual: these might seem poor grounds for hope in a world which is increasingly taken over by novelty and in a country where films count for more than *Nō* drama. But *sake* could be getting some unexpected support. Today the most popular films produced in Japan are about the *yakuza*, or honourable gangsters. And as in the American western — until recently, anyway — the consistent theme of the *yakuza* film has been the final victory of good over evil. The particular relevance of this universally attractive idea is that in these films the bad guys always come on in western suits and drinking British whisky or French brandy, but the good guys sip *sake* kimono-style. It's unfortunate, therefore, that one of the most popular *yakuza* stars contracted to do TV commercials for a Japanese beer company; but even a touch of consumer-schizophrenia would not come amiss at the moment, for whatever their packaging talents, *sake* manufacturers are novices when it comes to propaganda.

So, with the aid of the honourable gangsters the honourable drink might stage a come-back. And honourable it certainly is — it being the only drink in Japan whose name is often prefixed with the honorific *O-* (as in *O-sake*). But, as the gangsters suggest, perhaps the real threat to the return of *sake* is not the foreign liquors drunk by the bad guys, but their Japanese-bred cousins: Japanese beer, Japanese whisky and so on. The 'authentic' foreign brands are too expensive for the ordinary consumer, but the Japanese have succeeded rather well in producing relatively cheap — and still more relatively — good forms of foreign liquors. Japanese wine has not yet evolved very far, but the whisky is thoroughly acceptable, the brandy is coming on well, and in the opinion of many, Japanese beer compares favourably with its original German model. When the good *yakuza* sips a glass of Japanese whisky without taking off his *kimono*, then the foreign liquors really will have been naturalized and all *sake* manufacturers should commission a special drama of lament.

But this will probably never happen. Good *sake* is too good to die away and in any case the Japanese love acting out a fictional rôle. The fiction of social exchange between the customer and the *geisha*, who charmingly fill each other's *sake* cups; that amazing fiction-come-true world in which competitive Japan rediscovers human ritual, and where parties given to celebrate success can turn to spirited consolation, and consolation for failure can become a form of celebration — these all demand a delicate, gay and intimate atmosphere which only *sake* can create. Whisky is too impersonal for such occasions, brandy too straightforward. *Sake* mirrors and inspires that carefully balanced ambiguity of emotion which is what Japanese life is all about.

Chopsticks *by John Grisdale*

Who but the ceremonial-conscious Japanese would make common eating tools a symbol of veneration and an object of class-designated art?

Such is the rôle of chopsticks in Japan where there are probably as many types as there are tastes. From the commonplace split sticks of cheap untreated wood supplied in restaurants and noodle shops, sheathed in paper holders, to the cherished ivory, horn and mother-of-pearl inlay family treasures, there is no doubt that chopsticks are the simplest of eating tools. Emperor Hirohito, for example, prefers the traditional, untreated chopsticks (made from a kind of poplar) and favours the 21 centimetre long variety which he uses only once before passing them on to his retainers.

Ever-intensive industrialisation of Japan for over a hundred years has created both a shortage of wood and the actual artisans who work in the chopstick cottage industries. Though unrefined plastic chopsticks have entered the market as a stop-gap, they are irksome substitutes. Such victuals as slippery mountain potatoes or raw squid should be eaten with the aid of willow chopsticks. Handmade chopsticks are invariably superior as no machine can scrape along the grain of wood. And, like the *kimono*, there is today a revival boom in the use of chopsticks — contrary to the encroachments of western modes and manners.

According to Taro Nakayama, a well-known folklore scholar, chopsticks *(hashi)* originally used by the Japanese were a type of pincette, a pair of metal tweezers.

So *hashi* (without the honorific *O*) must have been named after the beaks of birds *(kuchi-bashi)* due to the similarity of shape and function. The old caricatured picture scroll, *Yamai-zashi*, shows two diners eating food with pincette-style chopsticks.

During the tenth and eleventh centuries only aristocrats used metal tweezer chopsticks (which were of Chinese origin), the plebeian masses using pincettes only for transferring food from a large communal bowl or dish to small individual ones; for the most part at that time everybody still ate food with their hands.

During the so-called Age of Wars in the following centuries, *samurai* knights were often compelled to eat their meals during intervals on the battlefield — a practice which might well have some connection with the lunch-box *(obento)* so popular today.

At that time superstition maintained that if foxes collected one thousand chopsticks thrown on the ground they (the foxes) would be transformed into human beings. At the same time the 1,000th *samurai* would thereby change into a fox. The knights not being brave enough to face this awesome risk (even if a white fox is sacred to the Shinto religion) broke and threw away their used chopsticks.

In olden times bamboo was used for chopsticks at formal banquets. It is a wood which has a beautifully refined texture and is used in so many folkcraft *(mingei)* products up to the present. Other woods used include willow, chestnut and bush clover branches as they were easy to sharpen. Pine and plum branches were also used, the bark left on where the sticks were held. In the post Middle Ages, upper-class *samurai* utilised lacquered as well as ivory chopsticks. In fact, chopsticks became more and more elaborate with the social élite and consequently more specialised and costly.

Half-split chopsticks *(waribashi)* are really quite a modern innovation (mid-nineteenth century) coinciding with the new prosperity and the custom of eating out. Restaurants had to come to terms with the need to prepare large quantities of packed food to take away, complete with cheap split chopsticks for throwing away after use.

In a country rich in folklore and festival it is not surprising that chopsticks are incorporated into various religious rites and superstitious ceremonies. One of the most fairytale-like and spectacular is held in the red and gold, lantern-lit Yasaka Shrine that dominates the Gion Quarter of Kyoto's *geisha*land.

This annual New Year's Eve Festival *(Okera Mairi)* utilises sawdust, or scrapings, from chopstick-makers' workshops mixed with an ancient Chinese medicinal herb, *okera,* to transmit a healing smoke which makes the surrounding air dry and is said to protect people from epidemics. In pre-modern times, in a country so prone to epidemics, this custom obviously had more practical significance than it does today. Swarms of people young and old from many parts of the country flood the precincts of Yasakajinja at this time.

For a small sum one can buy a small cord the end of which one ignites in the huge *okera-ohashi* incense flame. Still glowing, the cord is taken home in the early hours of the New Year, legend affirming its mystical power when one eats New Year's breakfast cooked by the flame lit by the cord. One would then be free from disease throughout the coming year.

Quite the oldest hereditary line of specialist chopstick-makers in Japan is the Ichiharasagami family business in Kyoto's commercial sector, whose dynasty goes back some 250 years.

At the end of the eighteenth century, the Palace authorised the new family name of Ichiharasagami, then, in the nineteenth century, it was contracted to Ichihara ('market field'). From its inception the Ichihara enterprise has been honoured by Royal patronage with orders from the Imperial household received to this day.

An Ichihara family heirloom is a picture scroll painted on silk by Goshun Matsumura entitled *Shirahashi no Okina,* the old white chopstick vendor who hawked his wares from place to place. He made wooden chopsticks from waste material thrown out by the Palace and sold them in town. This scroll hangs today in the somewhat conglomerated tiny Ichihara shop that stands dwarfed amid towering department stores and banks of main street Shijo in Kyoto's bustling city centre.

The Japanese attach special importance to the practice of eating together from the same pan, the food cooked over the same fire (e.g. *sukiyaki* and *nabemono*) to form a deep and unified human relationship. But it is simply not done to use communal chopsticks. Strict etiquette requires that the butt ends of chopsticks be used to secure portions of food from the common bowl or dish and never the tapered ends that have been in the mouth. One never uses another's chopsticks, even if washed, at a meal. Hygiene and delicacy of manners prevail always.

Aesthetically, compared with knives, forks and spoons which are basically hardware, chopsticks are light to handle, plain or decorative, graceful in use and warm to the touch. They lie poised together in parallel on a tiny ceramic block that itself can be a work of art. Western cutlery has changed its form many times, but chopsticks have remained constant for some 2,000 years in China, Korea, Vietnam and Japan.

Rice *by P. G. O'Neill*

It is no coincidence that the three main mealtimes in Japan are described in terms of *gohan*, literally 'honourable rice'. Breakfast is *asa gohan*, 'morning rice'; lunch is *hiru gohan*, 'midday rice'; and dinner is *ban gohan*, 'evening rice'. Rice, of course, has been the staple food of Japan since earliest times and *sake*, the wine made from it, has enhanced the meals and delighted the spirits for almost as long.

Because of the considerable variations in latitude and temperature down the length of Japan, the time sequences for rice planting and harvesting vary from place to place, but all parts of Japan have native Shinto ceremonies connected with the rice crop, and these are the most important of her agricultural festivals. Most of these ceremonies take place during the winter, when the short hours of daylight and the frozen ground allow little work to be done in the fields, or at planting time in the early spring and summer.

In wintertime, the farmers give thanks to the *kami* (gods) for the harvest that is past, and make plain to them their hopes for the one that is to come. Typically, they make their approaches to the gods by offerings of *sake*, food and fruit at the local Shinto shrine, and by the presentation of a wide variety of songs and dances for their entertainment. An equally important element of these winter festivals is the re-enactment of the year's crop cycle, also for the benefit of the gods who have been summoned to the shrine. Ploughing, harrowing, sowing, planting-out and harvesting are all depicted there, with the understanding that the gods being fêted will respond by ensuring that the real planting and harvesting are a similar success later in the year.

These ceremonies are traditionally carried out by men (according to Shinto beliefs, women are more likely to be ritually unclean), and often go on throughout the night, in the cold and discomfort of the winter countryside. In contrast, the spring planting festivals are warm and colourful occasions in which all the villagers, men, women and children, take part.

The standard form of a planting festival is for rice seedlings to be first blessed in a ceremony at a local shrine and then planted out in a paddy-field belonging to it which is known as the *shinden*, 'god-field'. The plants are often carried there from the shrine by children for, being innocent and ritually clean, they are regularly used in Shinto ceremonies as the messengers or representatives of the gods. The planting-out is done by young men and women of the locality, usually to the accompaniment of traditional music and dancing. Once the god-field is planted, the local people can go ahead with the same work on their own land, secure in the knowledge that the age-old safeguards against disaster have been suitably observed. Despite the great advances in farming techniques and the availability of modern scientific knowledge, there are still many farming families who could not plant their seedlings with confidence and easy minds unless the appropriate ceremonies had been carried out at the local shrines first. The past is a history of too many crop failures and too many famines for them to dismiss lightly the need for the blessings of the gods.

Plates 39 and 40: *Scenes from a rice-planting festival in Hiroshima Prefecture.*